Tackling A Level Projec in Computer Science

OCR A Level Computer Science H446

Ceredig Cattanach-Chell

Published by
PG Online Limited
The Old Coach House
35 Main Road
Tolpuddle
Dorset
DT2 7EW
United Kingdom
sales@pgonline.co.uk
www.pgonline.co.uk
2019

PG ONLINE

Preface

This guide to Tackling A Level Projects in Computer Science is designed to give you clear and focused advice to help you maximise your potential when completing your project.

It will take you through all aspects of the project, from document setup, to each stage of the process. This guide will give you tips, and clearly written support to:

- Help you create a professional looking report
- Outline what is required for each section of the documentation
- Help you to understand the exam board's requirements
- Give advice on how to meet these requirements
- Give you a checklist to help ensure you have completed all required parts of the project

Whilst this guide can be used to support any programming project, it is tailored to meet the requirements and expectations for the OCR A Level Computer Science (H446). It is therefore recommended that this guide is used alongside the specification you are following in addition to support from your Computer Science teacher.

You should make sure that the project you are proposing is challenging enough to meet the requirements of A Level. Your teacher should be able to support you in checking whether your proposed project has a broad enough scope to access all the marks.

Acknowledgements

Every effort has been made to trace and acknowledge ownership of copyright. The publishers will be happy to make any future amendments with copyright owners. The author and publisher would like to thank the following companies and individuals who granted permission for the use of their images in this textbook.

Chapter 4 Survey Monkey image: Sharaf Maksumov © / Shutterstock.com

Chapter 2 Word screenshots © Microsoft®

All other images © Shutterstock

First edition 2019
A catalogue entry for this book is available from the British Library
ISBN: 978-1-910523-19-3
Copyright © C Cattanach-Chell 2019

Printed on FSC® certified paper

Printed and bound in Great Britain by Bell & Bain Limited

Contents

Chapter 6 – Software development   67

Chapter 7 – Evaluation   80

Chapter 8 – Final checks   85

Index   89

Appendix   92

Chapter 1
Starting a new project

Objectives

- Choose a project title
- Choose a stakeholder
- Create a project outline
- Understand:
  - How to be realistic in your project scope
  - An appropriate level of difficulty for your project
  - Languages that are and are not appropriate to use
  - The design methodologies that could be used
  - Different options for IDEs
  - How your work is authenticated

Introduction

Choosing a suitable A Level project is quite a challenge. Projects contribute to your final grade and therefore choosing the right project for you is important.

This guide will take you through the steps to create a successful project. It will not give you the answers, but instead show you tips and tools to help keep you on track, and evidence your project efficiently. Using this guide and the specification should give you confidence in being able to produce the best project you can.

Projects are not about quantity, but quality. Exam boards have specific **mark schemes**. You need to show you meet each of the mark scheme points. Clear and precise documentation makes it easier for both you, your teacher and the moderator to identify where you have met **mark criteria**.

> TIP   Ensure that you fully understand the mark scheme before starting your project.

Chapter 1
Starting a new project

The most important advice that can be given when undertaking projects is:

1. You may be tempted to spend a lot of time programming and ignoring the documentation. However, your program is part of the project, not all of it.

2. Make sure you choose a project that is realistic, and one that you are capable of completing. If you are motivated to complete the project and find it interesting, then you will be more motivated to overcome any challenges that may present themselves.

3. Every section of the project depends on the **Analysis**. The Analysis is the first part of your project. It is worth spending time making sure this section is done as well as possible. Moving on too quickly may mean that you struggle to complete the Design, Implementation and Testing sections effectively.

> **WARNING** Many marks are given to your report. It is crucial that you work on this throughout your project.

Choosing a project title

A suitable A Level project requires you to think about:

- Your own confidence levels in programming
- Design strategies
- Time frames
- Exam board requirements
- Languages
- Project scope
- Stakeholders
- Available support

> **TIP** Think about what you may have done at GCSE. A Level projects must go beyond that level of challenge.

There are almost no restrictions on the types of project which are allowed. All of the following could make good A Level projects:

- Games
- Applying AI to solve a particular problem
- Mapping or route-finding applications
- Automation
- Use of Raspberry Pi or Arduino technology
- Data set analysis
- Using APIs to collate and analyse real-time data

The important focus should be on programming in a high-level text-based **programming language**. Your project must allow you to demonstrate your programming abilities, not just design a nice website, or use some SQL in a database.

The first step to a good project is generating good ideas. Your best idea may not be the first one you have. Take time to create a range of ideas.

TIP   Always take time to generate as many ideas as possible. Investigate the best ones, and then choose your project.

Generating many ideas may seem hard. However, almost anything can be made into a good project with some thought.

Try this process to create project ideas:

1. Write down a list of all the areas and interests that you have – try to produce 10
2. For each of these areas, write down potential problems you think you can solve
   a. Write down everything that you think of – you can review them later
   b. Spend at least 30 minutes doing this
   c. Aim to get 20-30 ideas
3. Come back a day later and check - add anything else you think of
4. Wait two days and then pick your favourite 10
5. Narrow these 10 ideas down to five. Try to use your teacher or friends to help
6. Take each of these five ideas and write a small project brief for each
   a. This should be three paragraphs or around 100 words
   b. Narrow down and develop the ideas further
   c. Try to add three main success criteria for each idea
7. Narrow the list down to just three ideas
8. Turn each of these ideas into a longer project proposal
9. Discuss the proposals with your teacher
   a. Check they have the potential to meet the requirements of the mark scheme
   b. Check they are realistic timewise
   c. Check you will have the resources to do each project
   d. It may be that your teacher can ask the exam board for advice at this stage if needed
10. Finally, choose the one idea you will take forward for your final project

TASK   Go through the idea generation steps above

Chapter 1

Starting a new project

Good project title examples

Project Title	Brief idea
Robot Navigation	• Create a learning algorithm to navigate a maze • Allow the robot to navigate a maze • Show that it learns, as each navigation should be faster • Allow it to deal with random obstacles
Twitter Crawler	• Scrape keywords from a user's Twitter feed • Build a profile of the user's interests • Search for other Twitter feeds with similar interests • Recommend feeds for the user to follow • Adapt based on the user's uptake of these suggestions
Dungeon Crawler	• Player vs Computer AI • Character navigates traps and challenges • Character is chased by AI dragons • Levels generated procedurally • AI adapts to player strategy • Online leader board system
Revision Quiz (Note: Be careful that quizzes have sufficient depth, such as illustrated here. Basic quizzes typically fall well short of the required depth.)	• Support candidates with revision • Log in and recording system • Database of questions linked to specification/exams • Self-adapting learning algorithms to modify quiz based on user answers • Predictive graphs to show progress and potential grades • Auto-generation of revision plans based on progress

The ideas above are good as they allow you to develop algorithms to an A Level standard. They require interfaces and will test your programming skills. Each project can also be implemented in an object-oriented manner which will help in the design and planning stages.

Project Title	Brief idea
Website	• Car website • Shows pictures of cars for sale • Users can search and browse for cars they want • Database of cars can be updated by manager
Stock system	• Record incoming stock • Allow customers to order stock • Say when stock items have run out • Print a receipt for a customer • Allow new stock items to be added • Print monthly invoices and receipts
Games Quiz	• Has a bank of questions • Asks questions at random • Allows user to select topic • Records player scores • Prints out best topic answers

These projects have potential to be good A Level projects – but do not go far enough in terms of depth.

Building websites with database back-ends are fine – but the idea should be to use more complex algorithms to process the data in better ways. The same problem exists with the stock system project proposal. Projects require programming in a high-level language. HTML and CSS will not meet this requirement, nor will SQL. JavaScript may be used here for some client-side functionality. Using a server-side language such as PHP will strengthen the use of a high-level language even further.

Some examples of how the ideas above could be developed further would be by incorporating auto-prediction, analysis of sales data, live updating or multi-user access.

Basic quizzes are, again, not deep enough for A Level. Compare the features with the revision quiz given earlier as an example of a good project.

Before any final decision is made, check again with your teacher that your project will allow you to access the marks you need from the mark scheme.

TIP	If you are unsure about your project idea, it may be possible to send it to OCR to get feedback on it. Ask your teacher about this.

Chapter 1

Starting a new project

Choosing stakeholders

A **stakeholder** is someone who may be interested in using the system but is not necessarily the person you are designing the system for.

The stakeholder you choose to use the system you create is very important.

When picking a stakeholder try to avoid:

1. Using your friends as stakeholders
2. Being your own stakeholder

Stakeholders may be used when you decide to create a program for your own needs. They are people who can help you scope the project and give you feedback on your ideas. This discussion is important to ensure that you have a range of ideas to draw on during the analysis.

> **TIP** Successful projects will have other people involved to help provide ideas, feedback and testing results.

Anyone can become involved in your project, but it is better to be careful who you choose. Try to avoid choosing your Computer Science teacher. However, another member of staff could work well as a stakeholder. For instance, if you are thinking of a fitness tracker then a member of staff in the PE department could make a good choice.

Choosing classmates or friends may seem like a good idea. However, if you do, you must be sure that they are willing and able to be critical of your system. When it comes to testing and evaluation you want your stakeholders to provide sensible and critical feedback, rather than simply stating that "it all works wonderfully".

The stakeholder must have the time to give to your project. They may say yes at first, but will they still be happy to help six months later? Let them know how much time will be required of them, and when. For instance, if you use a teacher, remember that many teachers have coursework or mock exams to mark which may be around the time that you want them to start testing your solution. This could affect your progress.

Try to have backup stakeholders. If your initial stakeholder finds that they cannot help you to the end of your project, then your backup ones will be able to step in. It won't be ideal, but it will be better than your project collapsing.

TIP	Ensure that the chosen stakeholder(s) are suitable, available and willing to give you their time. This is critical to project success.

Use the following table to see the benefits and drawbacks of using certain types of people as your stakeholder.

Stakeholder	Benefits	Drawbacks
Friends	• Generally good availability • Supportive	• Biased towards your project or you • May not have the experience you need • May be unwilling to criticise
Teachers	• Experienced in what you need • Impartial	• Can get very busy • May have multiple people asking them • Can have periods where they cannot help due to marking or similar
Family	• Likely to be available • Reliable	• Could be biased • May not have experience in the area of your project • May not be able to provide other ideas as solutions
Clients	• Know what they want • Able to be critical • Knowledge of the area they work in • Interest in the end product being functional	• May have periods when not available • May not be there for the lifetime of the project • May not be IT experts and demand more than is realistic • May ask for more as the project goes on

Being realistic

Very large projects may be unrealistic to achieve in the time you have. Often, picking projects which are too ambitious can lead to a mid-project collapse. If your project appears to be becoming too big, a good strategy is to define the core components of the system. Once you have defined these, then ask "What can I add on if I have time?". Thinking this way will remove some of the pressure and make the project more manageable.

> **TIP** It is better to do a smaller realistic project well than a more ambitious project badly. Of course, make sure that the project gives enough opportunity to demonstrate the skills required on the mark scheme.

Big projects will require significantly more testing. The designs will be more complex and the write up will become much longer. Focus on smaller projects which allow demonstration of the requirements set by OCR. Repeating the same skills many times may not gain you any extra marks but will increase the amount of work you have to do.

Plan how you will evidence your work to save time. Often only critical tests and failures need to be recorded during development to show how your system progressed.

Consider using **video evidence** for some testing. Video testing works well on tests for transitions, games and stakeholder interaction. Free screen capture software is available to help with this.

You should also plan where you will focus your time and effort. Check how many marks each section is worth in the mark scheme, then ensure that you give yourself enough time to complete each section well.

Larger projects need more drive and focus. Think how you react to being under pressure when things are not going well. Focus on projects that can be broken down into smaller parts and then merged.

Keep a project plan with **milestones**. It is important to use some sort of tracking system to help you meet your deadlines. It may be that if you see you are running out of time, that you can modify your system suitably. Try to think about this as you design your system.

> **TIP** Plan your project carefully. Build in some **contingency time** for unforeseen problems, then stick to your plan.

Appropriate difficulty

Choosing a project is a challenging task and depends on a range of aspects.

How confident are you at programming?

Think about your programming skill level. It is good to learn new things but consider how much time is available. If you cannot learn how to do a new skill, how will this affect the project?

If you are new to programming or find it difficult, you may want to focus on a smaller project which allows you to build the skills needed as well as meet the mark scheme criteria.

Systems that have no online capabilities and work on a local machine are usually a good start. Trying to interface with APIs or multi-user access systems may be too much to begin with.

For example, a simple player vs. computer game can give a lot of opportunity to show skills, and yet keep the concept quite simple.

What language are you using?

Using many languages may allow you to create a more complex project. However, it is also increasing the risk of failure and challenge within the project. Similarly, choosing to do a project in a language you have never used before will give you far more work to do and be riskier. Sometimes, using what you already know is the best approach.

Exam board requirements

The exam board has rules for the expected difficulty of projects, and it is important that these are met. However, if you are less confident in programming, you may choose to limit your project's technical aspects so that you can create a stronger project across the other sections.

Thinking modularly

It is a good idea to split your project into modules. Start with a core, which will allow you to demonstrate a good level of programming and skills. Then have **modules** that you can add to the project to help develop either its challenge, or function. Working this way allows milestones to be met. Your project can steadily be built up whilst meeting all sections of the mark scheme well.

> TIP
> Focus on the core elements of implementation and testing. Focusing on core evidence to meet the mark scheme will help keep your report short and easy to follow. There is no need to document absolutely everything – be selective.

Languages

There are many languages that can be used for a project. Some languages suit certain types of project more than others.

The majority of projects will be done in a high-level text-based language. Python, C#, Java and VB.NET are suitable languages that are commonly used. The exam board generally restricts you from using 'drag and drop' languages, such as GameMaker and Scratch.

> **TIP**
>
> OCR does not limit the high-level programming language(s) that can be used. If you want to use one which is not in the specification, then check with your teacher that it can be used. They will need to be confident that they can mark your work and they may also need to email OCR to check or ask for permission to use the language.

Design methodologies

There are three main ideas for design methodologies that you could use.

Waterfall

This is quite a fixed methodology. Over time it has become more flexible but runs more on the principle of completing each part of the project in step; for instance, completing an Analysis and then moving on to the Design. If you find issues whilst completing the Design, you have to move back to the Analysis section. Once the Design is done you move on to the Implementation. Again you may have to move back to the Design or Analysis if needed.

In this methodology you analyse the whole project, build the whole project, implement the whole project and finally test the whole project.

Benefits	Drawbacks
• Fixed requirements/analysis means less project creep • Easily understandable and clear, set phases to follow • Identifying bugs and issues early can save time	• Very structured so less flexible • Very linear • 100% dependent on a good analysis

Iterative/Agile

Iterative or **Agile** development methodologies are more likely to be used at A Level. This methodology uses short focused cycles of the waterfall methodology. For instance, you may do an iteration on the user interface, or an iteration on an AI feature.

The project will be broken down into sections — each one taking one, or many iterations. By its nature, iterative design is more flexible and it may be easier to alter ideas and change direction.

Iterative design still requires a clear idea of the end product. However, it deals better with unpredictable stakeholder requirements, or when the final product is initially hard to define. It also allows for more regular stakeholder feedback.

Benefits	Drawbacks
• Shorter and more focused sections of project completion • More flexible • Able to adapt to changes more quickly • Much more regular stakeholder interaction • Inconsistencies across your Analysis, Design and Implementation can be detected more easily • You can design each iteration to be of a similar size, which spreads the work out	• Stakeholder feedback too often can slow down the project • Additional ideas can creep in mid-project • May be harder to plan logically • Changes in one area may affect others and therefore you need to revisit those areas as well

Prototyping

Prototyping is used when your initial idea is formed, but the requirements are very vague and undefined. Prototyping allows you to build short and quick examples, which can be evaluated and refined as you go. This may then lead into iterative design once you have more idea as to the direction of the project.

Prototyping can achieve a working skeleton product very quickly. It is important to remember that this will not necessarily lead to a final, defined product. However, it will help in defining the final product, and give you useful feedback.

TIP	You may not be sure on an aspect of the solution that the stakeholder wants such as the user interface. You can prototype two versions and get feedback on them. Once you have the feedback, you can clarify and design the final version more confidently.

Benefits	Drawbacks
• Quick gains • No need for requirements to be fully scoped before starting • High level of stakeholder interaction • Final product is more likely to meet stakeholder needs • May result in faster products being produced	• Lack of analysis may mean misunderstanding in what is needed • Can get stuck redesigning the same area many times • May become difficult to define between a prototype and a finished component • Very easy to lose track of time, leading to late delivery of the final product

Choosing an Integrated Development Environment

The **Integrated Development Environment (IDE)** is the software in which you will enter and run your source code. Simple IDEs are often used at GCSE, for example you may have used IDLE at GCSE for Python programming.

A Level projects will require a significant programming element and choosing an IDE that will provide the support you need is worthwhile.

MS Visual Studio has many more in-built features to support you more than a simple IDE such as IDLE

Many IDEs contain the ability to create file structures, in-program help and support, links to developer communities and so on. Your IDE can either be a great support or add an extra level of challenge.

> **TIP**
>
> Some IDEs, such as Visual Studio provide the facility to easily create Graphical User Interfaces (GUIs). Choosing such an IDE early in your project may save you significant amounts of time later.

The options you have for your IDE will possibly be dependent on the programming language that you choose to use.

There are specific environments available for game making such as Unreal Engine or Unity.

Authentication of work

The declaration form

All work must be your own, authentic and free from **plagiarism**. You will be expected to sign a candidate declaration form stating this.

You may be allowed to work outside of supervised lessons. Your teacher may well ask you questions about work you have completed outside of lessons to make sure it is your own work.

Once you have signed your declaration and submitted work to the exam board, any questions over authenticity or evidence of plagiarism may result in a malpractice investigation. If found guilty, the consequences are severe and could lead to you being withdrawn from your A Levels.

> **TIP**
>
> Always record any resources that you refer to both at the point you use them and in the references section of your report.

With growing use of GitHub and other repositories, it is becoming easier to find code that fits your own specific needs. This should be referenced. Remember that if you did not code it, you are not going to get marks for it.

If you are stuck or need help, research techniques and not solutions. If you do use code from a source, referencing it and then showing how you have adapted it to your needs is essential for your teacher to award you marks fairly and accurately.

> **TIP**
>
> Researching programming techniques and then adapting them will get more marks than researching complete solutions.

Chapter 1
Starting a new project

To do list
Have you done the following?

☐ Chosen a project title

☐ Created a proposal for your project

☐ Considered if the difficulty and size of your proposed project is achievable

☐ Chosen your stakeholder(s)

☐ Chosen the programming language(s) you will use

☐ Chosen the IDE you will use

☐ Got your proposal approved by your teacher

☐ Created a project plan with milestones

Chapter 2
The report

Objectives

- Set up a template for your work
- Create your own headers, footers and styles
- Ensure essential information is shown on your document
- Understand and use referencing correctly

Setting up the document

When writing a report, there are requirements for what should be included in your report.

Key details need to be included on each page such as your **name**, **candidate number**, **centre number**, **qualification code** and **page number**. If the report is printed for any reason, this will help to identify it and ensure it is in the correct order.

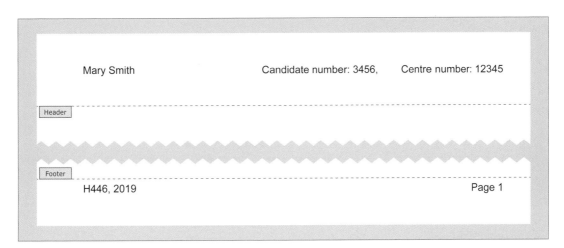

Chapter 2
The report

Word processing software

The best way to create the report is with word processing software. Using presentation software or other software packages is usually not appropriate. Learning how to use a word processing package effectively is key. It will also be a life-long skill.

Word processors have many tools to help you create neatly laid out documents. A well laid out document will be easier for your teacher to mark. It will also make it easier for the moderator to find evidence quickly when checking the marks awarded by your teacher.

The final report is best submitted as a PDF file. This ensures that it will look exactly the same on the moderator's computer as your own.

Some key features of word processing software that you will find useful in your project:
- Styles which can be used to auto-generate a contents page
- Headers and footers for your candidate details and page numbers
- Page and section breaks
- Tables, borders and shading
- Auto-referencing

Title page

Your title page should be functional. It does not need to be particularly fancy.

Title pages should have the following information:
- Full name
- Candidate number
- Centre name
- Centre number
- Project title
- Qualification code
- Date

There is no need to have more information than this.

> **TIP** The **cover page** does not get you extra credit, so do not spend long on creating it.

Many word processing packages have pre-designed cover pages and styles to use. It is worth looking to see if you like one. This will save you time creating your own.

> **TASK** Create a title page for your documentation

Selection of Microsoft® Word templates

Using styles

Styles are pre-set ways of formatting text. You should create and save any styles that are needed before adding any content to your document.

Using styles is important as they will be used later to create a table of contents for your work that will dynamically change as you add or delete pages. This will save you a lot of time.

Style options within a word processor

The most common ones you will need are Normal, Heading 1 and Heading 2. Again, there are no extra marks for creating styles. Use the default ones that your word processor or template provide.

You may find that there are certain situations where you need to create your own style. This will be most likely when you wish to add programming code to your report.

When setting up a style for code, remember that it is easiest to read if a **monospace font** is used. Copying and pasting code from the IDE that you use may also keep the **syntax highlighting**. This will make it easier for your teacher and moderator to read the code.

Use just one font for your report. This will make your report look more professional. To emphasise text or titles make use of font size, bold or italics. As mentioned, your code should be in a different monospace font.

TIP	Your styles should be clean and easy to read. The defaults that come with your word processor should be sufficient, so don't waste time creating your own styles other than for computer code.

TASK	Define styles for your document

Table of contents

A **table of contents** is essential for your documentation. It helps to show the teacher and moderator where your evidence is. Your teacher will use this to help reference their marking on the form that is sent to the exam board.

If you keep your work organised, a table of contents will also help you to refer back to tests, stakeholder success criteria and other parts of your report that you need to reference.

Most word processors will automatically create a table of contents. They make use of styles to produce these. It is essential that you are using styles throughout your report for this to work. Once set up, the table of contents and page numbers can be updated with just one click.

Word processors insert contents tables automatically
if styles have been used correctly

Keep your table of contents and page numbers up to date. It is worth updating the table of contents every time you close the document after working on it.

TASK Insert a table of contents after your cover page

Headers and footers

Headers and footers are repeated at the top and the bottom of each page in the report. They should contain the following items:

- Candidate name
- Centre name
- Project title

- Candidate number
- Centre number
- Page number

It is also possible to set up different headers and footers for different sections.

Using different section headers can be useful but they are not needed. If you understand section breaks then it may be worth using them. Otherwise, keep it simple.

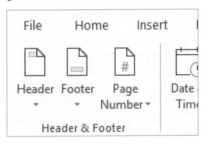

TASK Set up your header and footer for your document

Page numbers

Page numbers can be inserted automatically. Each page should be numbered. This is good practice and helps later when referencing evidence. They also help your teacher and moderator to find where evidence is located in the report. Positioning page numbers in the bottom right of the report is usually best.

Start the title page as page one. This will make the page numbers on the final **PDF version** of your report match those in Word. This will help your teacher and the moderator to navigate the report and any page references within it.

Chapter 2

The report

TASK   Ensure that your footer has page numbers in it

Referencing

Usually you will have unlimited access to resources. Therefore, it is important to **reference** any third party resources that are used for support within your project.

Using third party sources (e.g. ideas for code and technical support) is acceptable. Any use of sources **must** be referenced. You must also then show how they have been adapted for your project. This will allow your teacher to give you credit for how you modified the work from your source.

There are two ways to reference. The first is to put a superscript number next to the referenced work and then explain where it came from at the bottom of the page using footnotes.

The second way is to put the author's last name and year in brackets after the referenced work. Known as the **Harvard referencing** system, the full reference must then be written in a bibliography section at the end of your report.

The Harvard referencing system is the most commonly used referencing system, but there are others. There is no requirement to pick any one method. Whichever method you decide to use, it must be clear what sources you have used, and how you have used them.

Example of Harvard Referencing

"This piece of text has been taken from a Computer Science book" (Smith, 2019)

The copied text is put in quote marks followed by the authors name and year of publication in brackets. There will then be a full reference at the end of the project which looks like this:

Reeves, J. (2003). *An example Computer Science book title*. Publisher name, pg. 63

Smith, C. (2019). *An example Computer Science book title*. Publisher name, pg. 42

Tanner, B. (2016) *An example Computer Science book title*. Publisher name, pg. 184

An example of a reference in the bibliography section of the report

Using external sources effectively

If you do get stuck during your project, search for techniques and ideas, rather than for complete solutions to your problem. For instance, searching for 'Password Authentication System' and then copying code from a source will limit the marks that can be awarded. However, searching for a technique which can be adapted to your project will allow marks to be gained for the adaptation.

Similarly, a project should not be a record of how you followed a series of online videos to make a game. This will not gain you credit.

WARNING	Exam boards may use plagiarism software. Make sure you reference anything which you have quoted, copied or referred to.

Backups and versions

Your project will be completed over a long period of time and it will take several iterations. It is important to think about worst case scenario, such as.

1. Corruption of documents or program code
2. Loss of files on a school network or home computer
3. The need to go back to an older version of the project for evidence or due to issues in a newer version

Many promising projects have been unsuccessful due to students not giving careful thought as to how they will make backups and versions of their work.

Version control

You will complete your project incrementally. It therefore makes sense to save versions of your work at regular intervals. This will allow you to go back if you reach a critical error which cannot be corrected. It may allow two potential solutions to be created to see which works best. It is therefore important to have good version control when creating both your report and software.

When using **version control** ensure that each version is dated. It may also be useful to add a text file which briefly highlights important changes that were made in each version. This will make it easier to find the correct version later.

TIP	As a minimum, keep a version of your code at every major iteration and a version of your report after significant work has taken place or a section has been completed.

Chapter 2

The report

Name	Date modified	Type	Size
Project report Ver 1.docx	15/10/2019 15:55	Microsoft Word Document	17 KB
Project report Ver 2.docx	16/10/2019 15:56	Microsoft Word Document	92 KB
Project report Ver 3.docx	17/10/2019 12:32	Microsoft Word Document	463 KB

Different versions of a project report

Backups

Backups are similar to version control in that multiple backups allow you to keep a record your work. However, backups need to be kept away from the usual place that you are working. If you work at home, then the backup could be made on the school or college's system. **Cloud storage** and USB flash drives are other ways to backup work.

Make sure that there are at least two copies of all your versions of reports and software and that these are stored in at least two different locations.

How often you choose to back your work up is up to you, but it is important that it is done. Keeping a full back up of all your work each week is a sensible schedule, however, if you are doing a lot of work on your project, then a daily backup may be a good idea.

> **TASK** Find out what the backup policy is for files at school/college. Plan how you will manage your own version control and backup strategy. Write this below.

School/college backup policy: _____

My backup methods and locations: _____

My backup schedule:_____

To do list
Have you done the following?

- [ ] Set up a cover page
- [ ] Created a table of contents
- [ ] Created styles for the document (if necessary)
- [ ] Set up your header and footers
- [ ] Created a references section for your report
- [ ] Planned your version and backup strategy

Chapter 3
Stating the problem

Objectives

- Be able to describe the problem clearly
- Explain why this is a good problem for a computational solution
- Identify your stakeholders

The problem

Stating **the problem** forms part of the Analysis section of the report. It is where you will scope out your stakeholders, ensure your problem is suitable for a computational solution and explain how your solution will be able to meet the stakeholder's needs.

It is essential to be clear over the problem to be solved. It is just as important to know where your problem ends.

Defining the problem at the start is key to a good project. If you are not sure what is about to be solved, then issues will be encountered later. For instance, it will not be possible to give clear success criteria which will lead to further problems as the project progresses.

It is good practice to create a clear statement of the problem, the challenges that may be faced and a broad idea of what the system will do.

When doing this, think about whether the problem will be too big, or too small. Will it offer enough scope to meet the marking criteria for the project?

Be realistic. Well completed 'smaller' projects, that have enough scope to meet the marking criteria, often score as well as 'larger' projects that may have encountered problems along the way causing them not to be fully functional.

Define your limits for the project. If you think that some elements of the project could be added on at the end if you have time, state this. This is something you will be able to investigate in the Analysis section.

Chapter 3
Stating the problem

At this point you need to identify features of the problem that are solvable by **computational methods** and explain why the problem is amenable to a **computational approach**.

> TASK Create a clear description of the problem you aim to solve.

Describing the computational methods

It is important to state why you believe that your problem is suitable to be solved by a computer. The specification lists a range of computational methods that you may want to think about.

For example, it may be that the problem requires visualisation to show complex simulations such as the orbiting of planets or graphs of equations. In this case, parallel processing and speed could be considered. Use of **abstraction** could also be discussed.

> TIP Avoid generic advantages of a computation solution. For instance, if a chess game is being designed, stating that *"it allows a user to play without the need for a second human"* and *"it removes the need to carry a physical chess board"* will be preferable to generic statements.

In another problem that requires the calculation of a fastest route, specific algorithms such as Dijkstra's shortest path would be a useful computational method to consider.

The mark scheme asks for essential features to be explained. This means that this does not need to be a long section, but one that focuses on the most important parts.

> TIP It is important that you include this section in your work as the requirement is contained in all four mark bands of the Analysis section.

> TASK Describe and justify the features of the problem that are solvable by computational methods and explain why the problem is suited to a computational approach.

Stakeholders

Now list your **stakeholders**. State who they are, and how they interact with the **current** system. You do not need to investigate the problem at this point as this will be carried out and justified later in the Analysis section. You will, however, need to think how, or if your solution will suit their needs. This needs to be justified in the Analysis section.

Listing your stakeholders now gives you an opportunity to see how many people are involved in the problem, what roles they play, and the time that they can give you to help develop your project.

Stakeholder	Role	Interaction	Availability
Jenny	• Manager	• Stock reports • Sales performance • Hours record • Stock predictions • Price reviews	• Once a month
Dharit	• Sales Assistant	• Sales to customers • Hours logging • Review of targets	• Weekly
Sam	• Sales Assistant	• Sales to customers • Hours logging • Review of targets	• Weekly
Liu	• Sales Assistant	• Sales to customers • Hours logging • Review of targets	• Weekly

 Identify all the potential stakeholders of the system including their roles and interactions.

When completing the above task, you may want to consider the following questions:

1. Is there a good range of stakeholders?
2. Have all interests of stakeholders in the system been captured?
3. Will the availability of the stakeholders affect your project?
4. Will the stakeholders you choose be available until the project ends?
5. Do my stakeholders have the knowledge needed to help create the best system?

Stakeholders

Stakeholders are people who have an interest in the product. They may not necessarily be the end user. They may be individuals, groups or **persona**. For instance, in the above list of stakeholders you could show Dharit, Sam and Liu as separate stakeholders, or use just one persona of 'Sales Assistant'. If using persona, make sure that real people are still consulted to inform it.

Chapter 3
Stating the problem

*People who all have the same role
can be discussed as one persona*

You will need at least one stakeholder for this project. Stakeholders may also be people who can help advise on the system but may not be directly involved in the actual problem.

For instance, the system may need to be made suitable for people who are colour blind. Currently, no one who uses the system is colour blind, therefore, you could find someone external to act as a stakeholder and review your plans for supporting those who may have this condition.

Another example may be that the person you are designing the system for is not an IT expert. They may not know what features can be added to a new system. You may be able to find someone who could act as an advisor to help generate ideas and give you feedback on your plans.

To do list
Have you done the following?

- [ ] **Created a clear description of the problem**
- [ ] **Described and justified the features of the problem that are solvable by computational methods**
- [ ] **Explained why the problem lends itself well to a computational solution**
- [ ] **Identified and described the stakeholders in the solution**
- [ ] **Explained how the solution is appropriate to the needs of the stakeholders**

Chapter 4
The analysis

Objectives

- Research your problem thoroughly
- Use a range of research methods to collect data including:
  - Product research into similar problems
  - Meetings
  - Surveys
- Describe essential features and limitations of the solution to be developed
- Develop solution requirements for the system
  - Stakeholder requirements
  - Software and hardware requirements
- Develop measurable success criteria for the solution

Research

It is important to research the problem you aim to solve thoroughly. All projects should use **research** to help guide and support the requirements specification.

Research also forms part of the **marking criteria**. The requirements you define for your system must be fully justified. Discussions with your stakeholders will need to be undertaken to show the link between the initial problem and the requirements specification.

Chapter 4
The analysis

Qualitative and quantitative Research

Qualitative research produces data which is usually not numerical. This data must be interpreted, rather than putting it into a spreadsheet and trying to make a chart from it.

Quantitative research is usually focused on collecting numerical data which can be analysed through calculations or summations.

Which of these two questions would give you qualitative data?

"What are the most important features of the software?"

"Do you need a clock to be visible in the software at all times? Yes / No"

The first answer will be qualitative as there is a wide range of answers that could be given. Once the data is collected, it needs to be interpreted. For example, answers such as "I want something to click on to process an order" and "There should be an easy way to create an order" could be interpreted as "Button to process an order".

The second question is quantitative. There are only two answers, Yes or No. It would be possible to ask a number of stakeholders which they prefer and then analyse the data in a spreadsheet or with a chart.

Researching other solutions
The first way to meet the research requirements of the project is to analyse other systems that may exist. These systems will be solving a similar problem to the one which you are tackling. For instance, if you are making a 2D platform game, there are hundreds of existing games that could be used to show your stakeholders and get feedback on. They could be shown anything from gameplay, interfaces, graphics style or game themes and then comment on them.

When evidencing the research from other solutions, it is possible to include screenshots, diagrams or explanations of the solution. In some cases, it is then appropriate to add your own comments as to what you like or don't like. This can then be linked to how it will inform your own solution. The comments or views of your stakeholders are also very useful.

It may be that you think your idea is unique and that no other comparable systems exist. If this really is the case, then you should find systems that are as similar as possible or take different components from other systems that solve parts of your problem.

For example, a project requires a new game to be created using dice, cards and marbles. It is based around players taking turns with dice, and then battling with cards. The winner collects marbles that allow them to power-up either the dice or the cards.

In this case, you could research other card battling games such as Top Trumps® or Pokémon® for card designs and a description of the gameplay. Other games may then give ideas as to how the interface could look on a computer screen.

The same principle applies to any problem being researched and its potential solution. There will always be avenues of research which can influence your requirements list.

TIP	Be thorough throughout this part. Research similar solutions or ideas in depth. Justifying suitable approaches that could be used in your own product is the key to performing well in this section.

TASK	Identify other software or solutions that solve something similar to the problem you have or components of the solution you will be proposing. Include screenshots and diagrams where appropriate. Try to choose at least five different existing solutions to research.

TASK	Analyse the solutions you have chosen. What are their strengths or weaknesses? How could they be adapted for your solution? What opinions do your stakeholders have? Use your analysis and any stakeholder feedback to justify your solution's approach.

Meetings

Meeting your stakeholders is a great way to gain information. It also has drawbacks.

Benefits	Drawbacks
• Able to talk to people directly • Guaranteed meeting time • You can ask questions that you may not have thought of prior to the meeting • You can ask them for more detail instantly • You can get a better understanding of your stakeholders and their problem • You can build a relationship more easily • They may feel more confident in the project after meeting you	• You may need to travel • They may be hard to get hold of • They may be very busy • They may not give you as much time as you had hoped meaning the meeting is rushed • You need to be confident speaking to people face to face • They may cancel at the last minute leading to delays in your research • Too many meetings with one stakeholder may put them off

Chapter 4
The analysis

Balancing whether to meet stakeholders or not depends on many considerations. You may decide to meet one type of stakeholder, but then use a questionnaire or email for other stakeholders. For instance, in a system involving a salesperson and customers, it may be beneficial to meet the salesperson, but easier to collect information from customers by survey.

*Meetings with your stakeholder(s) are
essential to understand the problem*

TIP	Meetings take a lot of time to set up, but often get better quality data. Balance this with the effort required in organising many meetings and make each one worthwhile and focused.

TASK	Set up at least one meeting with your main stakeholder to discuss the problem. Record any ideas they have for the solution and any questions or points that have arisen in your research into other solutions.

Surveys

Surveys are a way of collecting data without needing to be present. They can be quickly created and are simple to send out, but they can be difficult to design well.

Some benefits and drawbacks of surveys are given below.

Benefits	Drawbacks
• Able to send to many people at once • Stakeholders can complete in their own time • May allow for quicker data capture • You can ask a range of questions • You can do them electronically or on paper • It may be easier to move into other software to analyse if done electronically • Some questionnaire platforms analyse data for you	• You must be sure you ask the right questions • Designing your questionnaire takes skill and time • People may miss the email or link • You will need to chase people to complete it • You cannot clarify questions immediately • You cannot always be sure all of the data entered is accurate • Paper based surveys need collating

Electronic surveys are very effective if you want to collect data from a large number of people, and the questions you want to ask are all the same for everyone. For example, if you are creating a game and need 20 people to answer some questions, a survey would be a great approach to take.

Designing a survey is challenging and not as easy as it first seems. However, many survey platforms have builders in them to help you create a good survey and test how effective it is before sending it out.

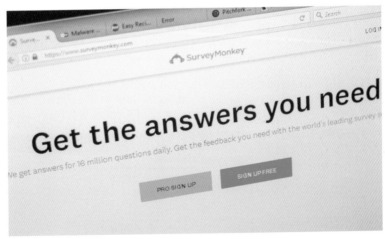

SurveyMonkey® is a free survey creator

TIP   When designing a survey, make sure you ask high-quality questions which gather the data you want to know.

Chapter 4
The analysis

Generally, it is more likely that you will use interviews first, and then follow up surveys to help clarify points and ideas you get from meetings. However, there is no right or wrong way.

It is important that you look at the time both you and your stakeholder(s) have available and plan appropriately. If you have questions for just one person it may be quicker to prepare a list of questions, and then ask them in a phone call, web conference, or Skype™ call instead of a meeting.

 TASK Plan your initial approach to your research. Choose whether you will use surveys, questionnaires, or voice/video calls. Then plan how you will both analyse the results and then follow these up afterwards.

Requirements

Requirements specification

The **requirements specification** defines the rest of the project. Each requirement should have some sort of research to support its inclusion in your project. Check to see that you have evidence to show why each requirement should be included.

When writing your requirements specification, it is a good idea to include some sort of numbering for each requirement. This will help you to reference them later in the project. It is useful, for each requirement, to refer back to evidence in your research that justifies the requirement.

Requirement		User Requirement	Solves	Evidence	Justification
		Log in screen	Secure entry to system	Pg. 4, Pg. 6	
1	1.1	Password Box	Requirement to enter password	Pg. 8	Secure entry t a log in scree username and
	1.2	Corporate colours	Fit company branding	Pg. 8, Pg. 9	The manager w professional to their company
	1.3	Auto clear option	Clear screen for security	Pg. 10	Various users t To ensure a 'cl clear' button s prevent errone

An example of part of a requirements specification

Once you have done this, you will also need to also **justify** your requirements. Consider how these requirements will be measured later in the project to demonstrate how they have been met. These are known as **success criteria**.

Further columns can be added to your table as follows:

ce	Justification	Success Criteria
g. 6		
	Secure entry to the system will be via a log in screen and users will have a username and password	• Required to enter password • Password is covered up • Will not accept passwords of less than 8 characters
g. 9	The manager wants the system to look professional to customers and fit in with their company branding	• Headers use Arial 16 pt. • Background is light grey • Font colour is Dark Blue • Manager confirms that colour scheme is appropriate
	Various users log into the system. To ensure a 'clear' log in screen, an 'auto clear' button should be used to help prevent erroneous log in at-tempts	• Button can be clicked to clear the screen • Screen automatically clears after 10 seconds

There are other ways to lay your requirements specification out. For example, here is an alternative method using a numbered list.

It makes sense to focus on 'sections' of the solution as demonstrated in the above examples which focus on the Login screen. This way you can break down these larger requirements into smaller and more measurable ones.

1. **Login Screen:** The user needs this to allow secure entry to the system, as described on Pg. 4 and Pg. 6 of the research. It must accept a username and password. There are several sub-criteria needed for this to be a success.

   1a. **Password Box:** The user wants a box to enter the password into which is secure. This was mentioned on Pg. 8.

   Success Criteria:
   - Required to enter password
   - Password is covered up
   - Will not accept passwords of less than 8 characters

Example of part of a requirements specification

For example, if you are making a game, then 'Game Interface' may be a requirement, which can be split into specific requirements for the layout, colours and content.

TIP	Break down the requirements into sections which then have small, precise and measurable requirements and success criteria.

If a single requirement is too big, it becomes very hard to include all the success criteria. By breaking down larger requirements, they become easier to deal with and it helps you to become more focused.

Measurable Requirements and success criteria

It is important that you can measure all your success criteria. Unmeasurable and vague criteria will not help you later when you come to test your system and prove that it works well. Some examples of measurable and vague requirements are given below.

Avoid stating obvious success criteria such as "The program shouldn't have bugs in".

Measurable requirements	Unmeasurable/vague requirements
• System should load within 10 seconds of opening the program • Colours should match the company's brand colours	• Should open quickly • Colours should be attractive to people who use the system • System should be stable

TASK	Create a list of numbered requirements for your system. Start with the main ones, and then break each main area into smaller ones. State what problem each requirement solves and link each one to research and a justification. Finally state the measurable success criteria for each requirement.

Identifying any limitations of the solution

It is important to state any **limitations** that the proposed system will have. Sometimes a stakeholder will make requests which are either outside the scope of the project, technically impossible, or will simply take too long to implement. Here, these limitations can be described. Include the justification for why you may have decided not to implement an aspect of the solution.

WARNING	Not implementing a feature because you do not know how to do it, or it is too complicated is not a good reason.

Explain any parts of the solution which will not or cannot be implemented. Justify why you have made this decision.

Hardware and software requirements

Considering hardware and software requirements is an important part of your project.

The **hardware and software requirements** may shape your solution, either because they limit how you can create the solution, or because the stakeholders may need to purchase additional hardware and software in order to use the solution.

Many A Level project solutions will run on a standard computer. If so, this is worth noting. However, you do not need to list a typical computer specification. The key is to mention any unique or additional hardware or software that is required for your system to be effective. This may be hardware such as sensors or bar code scanners, specific software, operating systems or libraries.

Recognising the additional hardware and software requirements will show that you have thought about the needs of the user, your solution and its success requirements.

*Remember to include hardware and software
requirements that will be required by your solution*

Create a list of all additional hardware and software that will be required to run the final solution that you build.

Chapter 4
The analysis

Commentary

Your commentary throughout your report should take both your teacher and the moderator through the journey to reach your final solution. It is not a specific section but runs through the whole project. Commentaries are written explanations of what, when and why you are doing something.

Quality is more important than quantity so be concise. Avoid writing 100 words when 10 would do.

Commentary for the Analysis section should show how you went from an initial idea for a problem, researched it, discussed it with the stakeholders, and reached your final decision for the solution.

Remember that there may be more than one way that the problem could have been solved. It may be that you thought both ideas were good, but your stakeholders chose one over the other or didn't mind either way. Always explain these moments.

Having other ideas 'in the background' is always a good idea. To start with, you will design and build the solution you feel will work best. However, if things go wrong, you will already have had a backup plan ready and waiting.

> **TIP** Do not become focused on the 'one' way you want to solve the problem. If things go wrong, Plan B and Plan C may be needed.

To do list
Have you done the following?

- [ ] Decided on methods of research for each stakeholder
- [ ] Planned interview questions
- [ ] Planned survey questions
- [ ] Decided how you will follow up your research
- [ ] Identified other existing systems or ideas you can research
- [ ] Discussed any suitable approaches to a solution
- [ ] Discussed and justified the chosen approach to the solution
- [ ] Created a requirements specification
- [ ] Justified each requirement based on the research evidence
- [ ] Stated measurable success criteria for each requirement
- [ ] Discussed any hardware and software that will be needed

Chapter 5
The design

Objectives

- Decompose the problem
- Explain the structure of the solution
- Design a solution to each part of the problem
- Use algorithms in the design of the solution
- Create suitable user interface designs
- List usability features for the solution
- Identify key variables, data structures, classes and validation
- Develop test plans for each part of the development
- Justify all decisions in the design process

Justifications

Justification is a key part of the Design section of the report. Initially, as part of **decomposition**, you will be breaking down the problem into smaller parts. The decisions you have taken for how the problem will be broken down will need to be justified.

When describing the design for the solution, you will need to explain:

- The structures you are using
- The algorithms used
- Key variables, data structures and classes
- Validation

All these decisions will need to be justified.

Some decisions will be easy to justify as they help to meet your requirements given in the requirements specification.

Being able to connect your design to your user requirements will help with testing and also support reviewing successes later in the project.

Chapter 5

The design

In many cases, justifications will show why a decision has been made from a Computer Science perspective. For instance, it may be because an algorithm is shown to be faster or a certain design of classes or data structures will allow for greater re-use of code should the solution need to be extended later.

It is therefore important that as you go through the Design section, continuous notes are written to justify choices.

> **TIP** If you cannot link parts of your design to your requirements specification, double check that they are required. Keep things as simple as possible.

Modular based design

Modular design takes large problems and divides them into sub-problems. Most sizeable projects are likely to use this approach and you probably used a similar design at GCSE level.

In order to make a modular design you will need to consider which parts of the problem can be made into specific **functions, procedures** or **classes**. For instance, you may need to consider "health" for both monsters and players in a game. Both will need the ability for the health to be removed or added to. These are likely to be implemented as functions (or methods) in your program.

Modular design is highly encouraged. In order to achieve it, you are likely to use two or more of the following diagrams as part of the solution's Design section:

- Decomposition diagrams
- Class diagrams
- Data Flow Diagrams (DFDs)
- Entity Relationship Diagrams (E-R Diagrams)

Decomposition

Decomposition is the technical term for splitting a large problem into smaller ones. Many people want to start programming far too early in the project. However, once errors arise or plans change, it can become very challenging to manage the code.

> **TIP** Having a clear breakdown of the problem will help you. Do not be tempted to skip this step.

Once you have split the problem up, it becomes easier to track progress through it. The smaller the chunks, the easier they may be to solve and manage.

Equally, testing smaller chunks more regularly will help to limit errors to just a small amount of code that needs to be fixed.

Breaking down the problem

Breaking down the problem is a useful way to turn your problem into smaller and more manageable parts.

Look back at the user requirements you have created. Which ones fit together or are linked? This may give a starting point for decomposing the problem.

Most break downs of the problem will use some style of decomposition diagram.

There is no right or wrong way of breaking down the problem. As such, there are several different methods of how this can be carried out shown on the following pages.

Decomposition diagrams

Many word processing packages have tools which can be used to create structure diagrams. The diagrams shown below were created using tools for organisation charts within Microsoft® Word.

Choose the method to lay out your diagram that you think works best for the decomposition of the problem that you are undertaking. Remember that these diagrams are only examples and your decomposition diagram is likely to contain more information.

Whilst these diagrams can be easy to create, careful consideration should be made at this stage so that the problem is decomposed into meaningful parts.

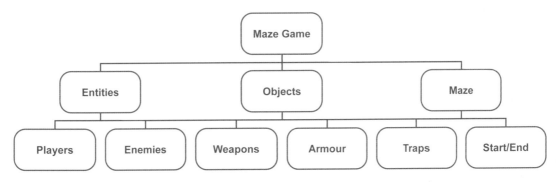

Example 1 - Decomposition diagram for a maze game

Chapter 5
The design

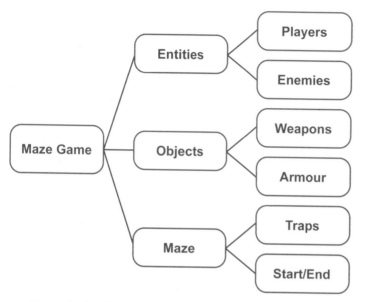

Example 2 - Decomposition diagram for a maze game

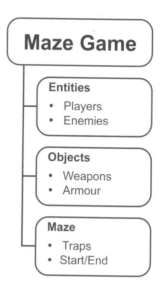

Example 3 - Decomposition diagram for a maze game

Lists

Using lists may be an easier option to set up. However, they can appear more complicated and become harder to track. If you decide to use a list, then be careful to make sure that the formatting clearly shows how the problem has been decomposed.

Maze Game

1. Entities
    a. Players
    b. Enemies
2. Objects
    a. Weapons
    b. Armour
3. Maze
    a. Traps
    b. Start/End

*Example 4 - Decomposition list
for a maze game*

Tables

Decomposition			Justification
	Entities	Players	
		Enemies	
	Objects	Weapons	
		Armour	
	Maze	Traps	
		Start/End	

Example 5 - Decomposition table for a maze game

Tables are easy to set up and you may find it easier to record these first in a spreadsheet. They also make better use of space than an organisational chart. This allows explanations and justifications of how the decomposition links back to the requirements specification to be added directly to the table.

Hand based drawings

If you prefer, you can draw decomposition diagrams by hand. These can then be photographed or scanned and added to the report. However, remember that drawing by hand can take longer and be harder to make changes to later. Be aware that if your solution changes, or you decide to restructure later, you will need to create a new version of the diagrams.

Versions

It is possible that you will find different ways that your problem can be decomposed. If so, include diagrams or written explanations of the different ideas. Then record the advantages and disadvantages of each method and justify the chosen way to decompose the problem.

Explanations and justifications

Once you have broken down the problem you need to make sure that you have explained and justified your decisions. Justifications of your decomposition will often reference the requirements specification, but there may also be a Computer Science related reason why you have chosen to break down the problem as you have – for example, it may enable you to use a library or algorithm you have found.

> TASK
> Create a decomposition diagram, list or table that shows how you have decomposed the problem. Give an explanation and justification as to why you have broken the problem down in the way you have.

Chapter 5
The design

Object-oriented design

Object-oriented design looks at creating entities known as objects which interact with each other. Each object can interact with another object, but only through specific ways.

Object-Oriented Programming (OOP) focuses on core ideas:

- **Inheritance** to help reusability
- **Polymorphism** for flexibility
- **Encapsulation** to keep states and behaviours within each object

If you plan on designing an object-orientated program, you must ensure that you develop the skills to do so. Object-oriented programming is part of the A Level specification. It is likely that most systems you create will tend to favour an object-oriented design, but not all will.

The following section looks at some of the key terminology and concepts of object-oriented programming.

Building object-oriented designs

Object orientation requires you to be able to spot common areas in parts of your problem that need a class to implement them.

Classes

Classes will be created as a 'template' for objects that you can identify within your design. For example, in a car racing game a Car would be one class which would store attributes such as `currentSpeed` and `maximumSpeed` along with methods (also known as behaviours) such as `increaseSpeed()` or `decreaseSpeed()`.

Player may be another class that stores information such as playerName and score.

The methods may be `getName()`, `setName(name)`, `addScore(amount)` and `getScore()`.

Looking at your decomposition may help to find areas of your problem that can make up different classes.

In object-oriented programming, the terms we use change a little from procedural programming.

Procedural programming	Object-oriented programming
Variables	Attributes
Procedures / functions	Methods

Objects

A class can be used to create multiple instances known as **objects**. This is known as an **instantiation** of a class.

Remember that the class forms a template that is re-used in making each object/instance. In the previous example of a car racing game, if three players played the game, there would be three instances of the `Player` class created for each of them. Each instance would have the same attributes and methods as the `Player` class. Each instance could then store a unique `playerName` and score for each given player.

> **TIP** Classes can be thought of as categories with objects being the specific instances. For instance, `Person` would be a class, whilst `Bob` and `Alice` would be instances.

Sub-classes

A class will match a certain category such as a Car class. It may be possible to make sub-categories from this. These are known as sub-classes. In the car game, the Car class stores `currentSpeed` and `maximumSpeed` as two attributes. Sub-classes could then be created for `PoliceCar`, `SportsCar` and `Taxi`. Each of these sub-classes would inherit these attributes, so they would each store the `currentSpeed` and `maximumSpeed`. The sub-classes could also have their own unique attributes and methods though. For example, the `PoliceCar` sub-class could have an attribute for `sirenState` with the methods `sirenOn()` and `sirenOff()`.

The process of a sub-class inheriting attributes or methods from its **parent** class is known as **inheritance**.

> **QUESTION** A quiz game is to be designed for a school classroom that one or more students and teachers can play. Any teacher can ask a question and any student can then respond. How could classes and sub-classes be used in the solution?

A class could be made called `Person`. This might store the name of each person and the time that they join the game (`timeJoined`) as attributes. The methods might be `getTimeJoined()`, `getName()` and `setName()`.

Two sub-classes could then be created. The `Teacher` sub-class might contain the method `setQuestion(question)`. The `Student` sub-class may have the method `answerQuestion(answer)`.

Both `Teacher` and `Student` sub-classes would inherit the methods and attributes from the `Person` class, so they would also be able to use the methods `getTimeJoined()`, `getName()` and `setName()`.

Analysis with object-oriented design

Identifying objects, attributes and behaviours

Identifying objects

Objects are often the nouns in your system. Take an estate agent, for example. House, Agent and Buyer are all nouns and could well form classes or sub-classes.

Identifying attributes

Attributes may also be called properties or class variables. Attributes store the values that are encapsulated in an object. Attributes of a `House` would be things such as `numberOfBedrooms` and `price`. Attributes will be shown inside a class on a class diagram.

Identifying behaviours

Behaviours are the methods that a Class can perform. A behaviour of the `Agent` class may be 'Sell House'. This may be implemented by the method `sellHouse()`. Behaviours of the `Buyer` class may be `setMaxPrice()` and `setMinPrice()`.

> **TIP** Remember that OOP design is a broad subject and other sources of information will go into more depth on the subject.

Class diagrams

Class diagrams are a standard way of showing an object-oriented design. They are drawn using **Unified Modelling Language (UML)**.

Class diagrams will show you:
1. Each of the classes used
2. The attributes available within each class
3. The methods available within each class
4. Whether classes are sub-classes, and inherit attributes and methods from a parent class

UML has many notations within it and an in-depth look is beyond the scope of this book. However, there are many websites available giving tutorials and explanations of UML.

The basic building block of a class diagram is an individual class.

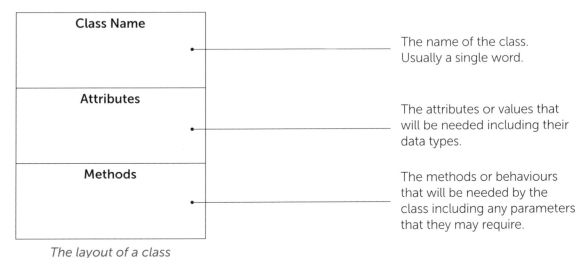

Class Name	The name of the class. Usually a single word.
Attributes	The attributes or values that will be needed including their data types.
Methods	The methods or behaviours that will be needed by the class including any parameters that they may require.

The layout of a class

Worked example of class diagrams

This worked example will consider a battleships style game and assume that the initial analysis of the problem has already been carried out.

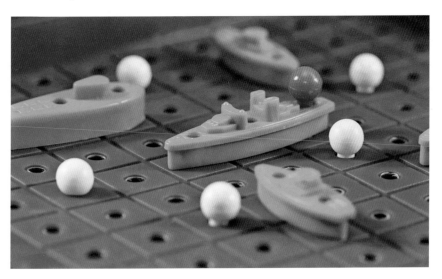

Chapter 5
The design

First, start with a class diagram for the Ship class:

Ship
shipType : String
shipLength : int
shipLocation: int[]
shipOrientation: Char
setOrientation: Char
setShipLocation(int[])
getShipType()
getShipLength()
getShipLocation()
getShipOrientation()
hitShip(int[])

An example of one class

WARNING The diagrams shown in this section are examples only and do not form a full system.

This diagram shows us that we need to create a class called Ship. It will have four attributes which store the data for the type of the ship, the length of the ship, the location of the ship and its orientation which will be either horizontal ('h') or vertical ('v').

Each attribute has a data type shown in the diagram and includes a string, an integer, an array of integers and a Boolean type.

There are two methods shown for setting the attributes. These methods are very simple and just allow the values stored in the attributes to be changed. They also show the parameters that may need to be passed to the methods. `hitShip(location)` by contrast is a method that can be called when the ship is hit. The class diagram doesn't show the algorithm that will be used for the methods, but it does show what methods the class will need to have programmed.

Sub-classes and inheritance

There are different types of ship in the game. These include a carrier, battleship and submarine. Each of these ships will have many of the same features as the `Ship` class, so we can use **inheritance** to create subclasses. The subclasses will have all the same attributes and methods of the parent class, but they can also add new ones that are unique to the particular subclass.

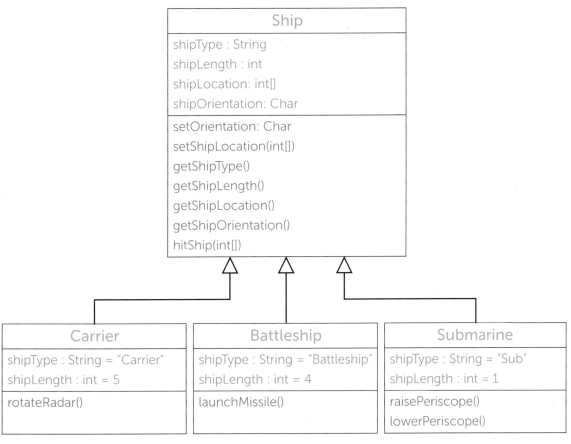

Three subclasses of the Ship class showing inheritance

Chapter 5
The design

Association links and multiplicity

A Board class can be added which will store where ships are placed and control what happens when they are hit. 1 board has exactly 5 ships, so these numbers can be written by the **association link**. Note that in the real game, two boards would be needed, one for each player.

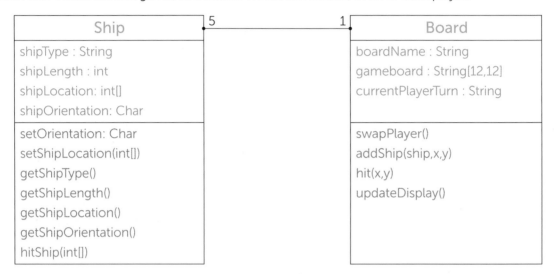

The number of instances that are created from each class is known as **multiplicity**.

0..1	No instances or one instance
1	Exactly one instance
0..*	Zero or more instances
1..*	One or more instances
*	Any number of instances
4..6	4 to 6 instances
3	Exactly 3 instances

Possible multiplicity instances

Further classes would need to be built for other objects in the game such as the players.

 If your project will make use of object-oriented programming techniques then create a class diagram to describe the system. Include any justifications for decisions you have made.

Database design

Many systems will rely on a database to store data. Design the database structure or schema is before it is built.

> **TIP** For more complex databases, you must understand the relevant database theory such as normalisation before you design the structure.

There are some key considerations to designing databases:

1. ### Data storage
   Although a project may need to store data, it doesn't mean that a database is required. Some data storage could be done through a simple file storage method. However, systems such as stock storage, orders and bookings will likely need the more complex facilities of a database.

2. ### Data relationships
   If the database required has more than one table then it is likely that there will be relationships between the data. Most database designs will need to be normalised to remove data redundancy.

3. ### Database-program connections
   There must be a way to connect your main program to the database. In some cases this is easy, but in others it may be more complex. You will also need to be confident in writing SQL statements for database queries.

4. ### Database design
   Database design will require the creation of one or more **Entity Relationship (E-R) diagrams**.

Chapter 5
The design

SQL

SQL stands for **Structured Query Language**. Knowledge of this language will be needed in order to access data from a database.

There are many GUIs that can connect to a Database Management System (DBMS) to simplify the task of building the tables. For example, MySQL® Workbench can be used with the popular MySQL DBMS. Similarly, Microsoft® Access® has a GUI to accompany its DBMS.

Remember that SQL isn't considered a *programming* language. It is a **query language** which can be used in your project, but you must make use of a text language such as C#, VB or Python. Use languages such as these to connect to a database if one is required. SQL can then be used to make necessary queries to the database.

TIP	Marks are gained for showing how a programming language and SQL have been used to add, edit, store and retrieve information from a database. Marks are not given for creating the database, so you can save time by using a program such as Microsoft Access to do this.

SQL syntax

A full consideration of SQL is beyond the scope of this book, however, some key terms are given below for reference.

SQL Command	Meaning	SQL Command	Effect
SELECT	Selects specific records from the table that meet certain criteria	**OR**	For a match, one or the other criteria are needed
FROM	Identifies which table the records will come from	**DELETE**	Used to delete data from a database table
WHERE	Adds the criteria that records returned need to meet	**INSERT INTO**	Used to add data to a database table
LIKE	Used to match patterns with the wildcards % (for zero, one or many characters) and _ (for a single character)	**JOIN**	Allows you to select data from multiple tables at once
AND	For a match, both criteria are needed	**UPDATE**	Allows records to be updated – used with the SET keyword

Basic queries tend to be written in the style:

SELECT column1, column2, column3 FROM tableName WHERE criteria

For example: `SELECT customerID, name FROM sales WHERE spend > 200`

Multi-table databases

At A Level, you are likely to need a multi-table database. This will need to be normalised and typically will be in **3rd Normal Form (3NF)**. Queries used will ideally use multiple tables and potentially involve aggregation of the data as well in some way.

Both SQL and Normalisation are topics within the A Level specification.

Carefully consider the database design before any implementation. Well organised data can be retrieved easily and help your program to work effectively.

Data tables

Data tables will show the core properties of each field in your database, as well as the table name and keys used. Each table should have a data table associated with it.

There are several important things to show in your data tables:

1. Table name
2. Field names
3. Primary key
4. Any secondary or foreign keys
5. Data types
6. Validation

Data tables can be set up quite easily in a word processor as the following example shows:

Table: Customer				
Field	**Key**	**Data Type**	**Validation**	**Notes**
Customer_ID	Primary	Number		
Name		String	1-20	
Surname		String	1-40	
Address		String	1-100	
Date_Of_Birth		Date/Time	<TODAY ()	
Postcode		String	5-8 chars Input Mask	
Email		String	>5 Include '@'	

An example of a data table for a Customer table

TASK If you will be using a database to store data, create a data table for each table you will need. Remember to justify any decisions you made.

Chapter 5
The design

Entity relationship diagrams

Entity Relationship (E-R) diagrams should be made for any database that will be created.

The minimum requirement for an Entity Relationship diagram will be that it shows all the **entities** (tables) and the **relationships** between them. Relationships will be given as **one-to-one, one-to-many** and **many-to-many**. E-R diagrams can also contain **attributes** (field names) that are associated with particular entities.

The following example is a simple E-R diagram for an ordering system. A customer has one order which contains many line items. Each order line contains a single item but an item may be ordered more than once on a different line or a different order.

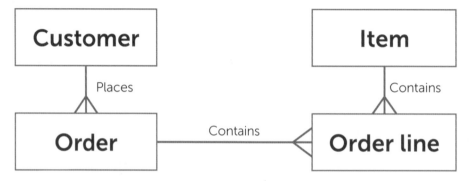

A simple E-R diagram for an online ordering system

 TASK — If you will be using a database to store data, create an E-R diagram. Remember to justify any decisions you made.

Data Flow Diagrams

Data Flow Diagrams (DFDs) show the inputs, outputs and how data moves within your system.

Data stores are the databases or files within the system. In the analysis, the users of the system will have been identified along with the actions which they will carry out.

Here is an example of a very simple Data Flow Diagram for a student registering on to a course in a school:

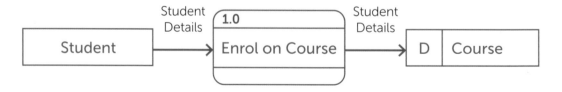

This shows that a student would pass their details to a process called 'Enrol on Course'. This process would then store the details in the 'Course' database.

A DFD for a school management system would be much more complicated in real life. DFDs may be time consuming to draw but will help to show how data moves within your system.

DFDs will require more understanding of database design. This, linked with how long they may take to design, should be a consideration. If your system is very simple, you may decide a simple E-R Diagram will be sufficient.

> **TIP**
>
> There are many diagrams that can help with the design of databases. Doing all of these for a large system may take a lot of time. You may wish to discuss with your teacher how much depth you need to go into to perform well.

> **TASK**
>
> Create a DFD to show how data will flow through your system. Remember to justify any decisions you made.

Algorithms

It is important that all **algorithms** for the solution are designed accurately and appropriately. The algorithms must together form a complete solution to the problem.

The aim is to create a collection of algorithms that would allow a developer to create the system without you.

> **TIP**
>
> Algorithms do not all need to be perfect at the start of the design process, but they should be correct before the final iteration is started.

Each algorithm may be hard to design at first without knowing how the other algorithms will function. It may be that there are two ways to solve a problem, and that it is not obvious which will work best.

A good design will show how all the **key aspects** will work.

Remember that this is a project that will be developed iteratively. You will have an overall set of ideas in the design section, but small sections of work will be incrementally built and tested. On each iteration, there may be small changes which affect other parts of the solution. This may mean that these parts need to be re-designed.

A completed algorithm design should be in **pseudocode** – and where possible as close to a real programming language as possible.

Chapter 5
The design

Algorithm design

Algorithms can be described in a number of different ways. Typically, a style of pseudocode that is similar to program code will be the easiest to use later in the implementation stage.

Some complex algorithms may require explanations of how they work in English or a flow chart to make them easier to understand. However, typically you will only need to use one of the following methods for your algorithm designs.

> **TIP** The method used to show algorithms for the solutions is up to you. What is important is that the algorithms presented are appropriate and accurate.

The following are examples of how algorithms can be shown in the Design section for a simple algorithm that will multiply two numbers together. This algorithm is purposefully very simple to show the different styles that can be used to present it. The algorithms you produce will be far more complex.

Pseudocode using loose English

> This algorithm will need to take two numbers as inputs and multiply them together. The result will then be returned to the main program.

Pseudocode using a flow diagram

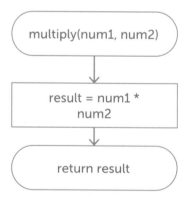

Pseudocode

```
function multiply(num1:int, num2:int)
        result = num1 * num2
        return result
end multiply
```

> **TIP** Try to use monospaced fonts when writing pseudocode.

Improving algorithms

Once an iteration has been implemented you may find that an algorithm needs to change. If this is the case make sure that it is recorded in the report.

After testing my 'multiply' method I noticed that it was causing an error.

```
multiply(num1:int, num2:int)
      result = num1 * num2
      return result
end multiply
```

This algorithm returned was using integers which when implemented in my program caused it to have an error as it needed to work with floating point numbers. Therefore, I changed my algorithm design to use floating point numbers, as shown below:

```
multiply(num1:float, num2:float)
      result = num1 * num2
      return result
end multiply
```

This new algorithm fixed the error as you can see from the code below:

```
27      0 references
        static float multiply(float num1, float num2)
28      {
29          float result = num1 * num2;
30          return result;
31      }
```

An example of how an algorithm can be updated if an error is found

> **TIP** The symbols used for flow diagrams must be used correctly. There is, however, no standard pseudocode style. The pseudocode that you write should be written in a manner that can easily be understood by another programmer.

Showing you have a complete system

You have already decomposed your system and shown the core structures needed to make it work. It is essential that these core parts all have algorithms designed for them. For instance, missing pseudocode for a core class in an OOP design will lose you marks. Missing an algorithm for an insignificant method within a class may not be as serious.

> **TASK** Create algorithms that describe the solution fully. These must be appropriate and accurate. Justify how these algorithms form a complete solution to the problem.

Chapter 5
The design

Using libraries and APIs

It is possible that the solution you produce makes use of built in libraries and APIs. Projects such as this are often likely to be strong and have a good depth to them.

> **TIP** Using libraries and APIs is allowed but your project will be judged on the code that you have written yourself.

Ensure that your project does not rely solely on pre-generated libraries or APIs to work, as this may limit the credit that you can be given in both the Design and Development sections.

Data structures and advanced techniques

Identifying and justifying your use of **data structures** is a significant aspect of the design section. At the simplest level, you must identify key **variables** that will be used in the project along with any **validation** that will be carried out on them.

Diagrams which explain database structures or class diagrams will help in showing that data structures have been considered. Some other data structures which may be considered include:

- Stacks
- Queues
- Graphs
- Lists
- Tuples
- Hash tables

Each of these data structures have standard ways of being represented. If your project requires these structures, show the structure and then illustrate it in your report with sample data as necessary.

Remember that you need to justify your decisions. For instance, the use of a queue may be appropriate to determine the next player in a game due to the way the data structure provides the facility to add (enqueue) a new player to the queue and remove (dequeue) the player at the front of the queue.

Justifications for other data structures, classes or databases may include the simplicity of the program required, speed of execution or requirements for re-usability.

Some programming languages may already have libraries for data structures that are needed. Show how you will use these, and how they will support your system. Remember you will also need to test that these work within your system – so do not forget to include them in your test plan.

Identify any key variables and data structures that will be used in your system. Remember to justify any decisions you made.

User interface designs

Usually it is a requirement that A Level projects will need a **Graphical User Interface (GUI)**. A GUI helps the user interact with the program. In a game, this will be the menu system and the placement of objects such as health bars and scores. For other systems, it may be where users enter data, view results and have menu bars placed.

The GUI is an important part of a project and should be accurately sketched out.

You should have researched features of GUIs for similar software to that which you are designing in the Analysis section. Make sure your designs reference any applicable research that was carried out earlier.

Wire frames are a good way of designing your GUI. These are line drawings. They will help to show key features and layout clearly. Specific aspects can be numbered and explained in more detail.

If you have key themes or **house styles** that must be used in the requirements specification, then refer to these here.

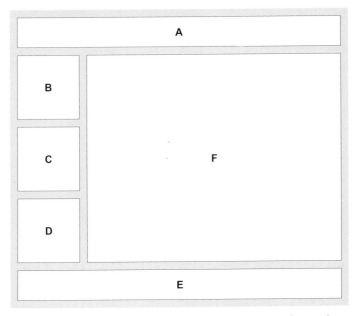

A: Page header

B, C, D: Advertising

E: Page Footer

F: Page Content

Styles
Header:
- Arial Bold 14pt, Blue

Page text:
- Arial 12pt, Dark grey

Page Header:
- Arial Bold 14pt, Black

Sample GUI layout for web page

Chapter 5

The design

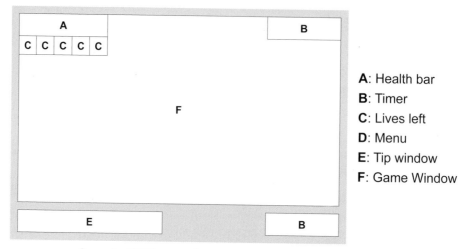

A: Health bar
B: Timer
C: Lives left
D: Menu
E: Tip window
F: Game Window

Sample GUI layout for web page

The sample GUI layout above is for a platform game.

This is a quick GUI layout for a side-scrolling game played on a PC. Whilst this did not take long to create, it shows the core elements of the GUI and is clear and easy to follow.

TIP	Create your designs in enough detail so that someone else could create them. This does not mean they have to be works of art.

You may wish to create your designs by hand.

GUI components such as scroll bars, check boxes or menus are useful to add in detail. In some cases, these may restrict inputs and therefore help in showing validation of inputs.

TASK	Create designs for the user interface.

Usability features

Usability focuses on these questions:

1. What makes your program accessible to the user?
2. What allows them to use your program more easily?
3. What have you found out in your research which will help a user understand, navigate and control your program?

The Design section should consider usability. This will link directly to any designs for a GUI that you may have already discussed. It may also reference other features you have added to help or support a stakeholder use your system.

Usability features may include the following:

- Ability to enter data again without the program crashing
- Colours and fonts to help highlight core information
- Layout of the GUI at certain points (e.g. enlarging boxes where data needs to be entered)
- Location of core elements such as menus and controls
- Text to speech options
- Ideas to help specific users, e.g.:
  - Colour blind users
  - Visually impaired users

You should link your usability features to the requirements specification in the Analysis. Doing this will help in justifying the choices that you have made.

Inclusion of usability features will help
make a system easier to use

TASK Add a section to your report on usability features. Link these to the requirements specification to justify your choices.

Chapter 5
The design

Test plans

The next stage in the Design section is to think about how the system will be **tested** to ensure that it meets the requirements specification and success criteria laid out in the Analysis.

There are two sections to your test plans:

1. Iterative testing
2. Post-development testing

These tests are different to each other in nature and therefore require different styles of tests.

Testing **must** be planned before any implementation, but you do not need to plan all the testing in one go.

It is perfectly acceptable to plan tests before each iteration. The implementation of the iteration can then be implemented and tested. Once the iteration works successfully, the tests for the next iteration can be defined.

Iterative testing of the solution uses **white-box testing**. This means that the tests are based on the code that is written. It is useful for checking that individual algorithms or sections of the program are working correctly.

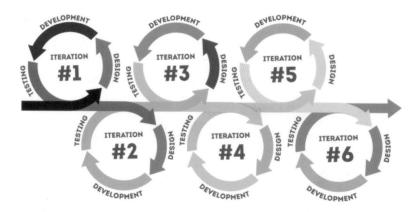

Remember that projects are usually developed iteratively. For each iteration, a short test plan is written before development is carried out.

Post-development testing is a form of **black-box testing** which is carried out once the entire solution is complete. It is possible to plan post-development testing in the design section before any implementation has been started. Your system designs could change as the project progresses, so remember before you start such testing to check that the tests are still valid and reflect any updates.

Remember that good test plans are designed to try and make the system fail. They should test that your system stands up to unintended use, and possibly malicious attack.

What needs to be tested?

Syntax errors

Syntax errors are normally detected by the IDE as the program is written or when the program is compiled. This type of error does not need a plan, therefore you will not need to test for syntax errors. You may record the more interesting errors and how they were fixed.

Logical Errors

All logic paths through the program should be tested. Check where Boolean expressions have been used and then write tests that will demonstrate that all paths through the code work in the way you expect. Will inputs to any algorithms, functions or procedures give the correct outputs. Logic errors will not usually be found by an IDE so it is crucial that a test plan is created with the expected results manually calculated and compared with the system outputs to discover them.

Runtime Errors

Runtime errors occur when the program is running, and unexpected events happen. It may be that certain inputs cause a 'divide by zero' error which hasn't been considered. Another problem may be that an inappropriate algorithm causes a program to run out of memory. Remember when writing test plans to consider parts of the program that may lead to runtime errors. For instance, if division is used, are there any inputs that need to be tested to see if they cause a runtime error.

Validation

Any validation rules that have been planned or implemented need to be tested. There are four types of test data that will need to be used:

- **Normal** test data should be accepted by validation rules without causing errors.
- **Boundary** test data checks the maximum and minimum values that may be entered. The data tested will be of the correct data type.
- **Invalid** test data is data of the correct data type, but just outside the validation rules.
- **Erroneous** test data should not be accepted. It will be of the wrong data type.

Good programs should detect and process both erroneous and invalid data and give the user a useful message as to the problem.

TIP You will need your tests to show that the requirements in the requirements specification have been met successfully. Each test should refer back to the one or more requirements as justification for their need.

Output

Output as a result will show you where errors may exist. It is possible that each function or class you test works individually but causes errors when linked to other functions.

Output checks will indicate where these errors may lie but may not show you exactly what is causing the error.

Chapter 5
The design

Iterative testing

Iterative testing is focused on the system itself functioning. For instance, if a function is created that is meant to multiply two numbers, iterative testing would need to check that the two numbers are correctly multiplied together and returned.

As stated before, the testing that you carry out for each iteration is also known as 'white-box' testing. This is testing which looks 'inside the box'. It checks functions, procedures and algorithms to see that they are working correctly.

White-box testing will often check parts of the program that the user doesn't see, such as if objects are working correctly or functions are returning the correct values.

Worked example

Consider the simple function that was created earlier:

```
                      0 references
27                    static float multiply(float num1, float num2)
28                    {
29                        float result = num1 * num2;
30                        return result;
31                    }
```

This now needs to be tested thoroughly to see that it works correctly.

Remember to consider test cases for:

- Normal data
- Boundary data
- Invalid data
- Erroneous data

At first, this may seem like a simple function to test. However, there are two parameters and each one will need to be tested. As both values are needed to run the function, we will have to create two input data items for each test.

This function also has no input or output from the user. So additional lines of code will be needed to test it.

ID	Testing	Type	Data	Expected
1	Both parameters are passed successfully	N	num1 = 1 num2 = 2	2
2	One parameter is text	E	num1 = 1 num2 = text	Error thrown
3	Decimal passed as a parameter	N	num1 = 1 num2 = 2.5	2.5
4	Negative numbers accepted	N	num1 = 1 num2 = -2	-2
5	Only num1 is passed to function	E	num1 = 1 num2 = no value	Error thrown

Possible tests for the multiply function

Some of these tests may not be required. For instance, if this function were to be called by another part of your program that uses variables which are already validated then it would not be necessary to consider all these test cases.

Testing the function

The following process shows how the function can be tested after the implementation of an iteration. The code below is written in C#. Five test cases have been placed at the start of the program to call the multiply function with the different inputs in the test table.

```
static void Main(string[] args)
{
    Console.WriteLine("Testing multiply function");
    //Test 1
    Console.WriteLine(multiply(1, 2));
    //Test 2
    Console.WriteLine(multiply(1, "text"));
    //Test 3
    Console.WriteLine(multiply(1, 2.5f)); //2.5f means a float value of 2.5
    //Test 4
    Console.WriteLine(multiply(1, -2));
    //Test 5
    Console.WriteLine(multiply(1, null));
}

5 references
static float multiply(float num1, float num2)
{
    float result = num1 * num2;
    return result;
}
```

Creating five test cases for the multiply function

As C# is a strictly typed language, the IDE detects the wrong data type for both "text" and null.

> **TIP** If you know certain tests will not be allowed to run because your IDE will detect them, then mention this. There is then no need to test these later.

Of course, if the user could input the erroneous data then the error will need to be caught before the multiply function is called. This will need to be tested.

Tests 2 and 5 can now be commented out so that only tests 1, 3 and 4 will be run.

```
Testing multiply function
2
2.5
-2
```

Output from testing the multiply function

The outputs match the expected outputs, so the tests have all passed.

Iterative testing must show that your system functions and is robust. Your test plans should cover all major components. The testing section of your project must leave the examiner convinced that your system works.

> **TASK** Create test plans for the algorithms that you intend to implement. Remember that test plans can be created for each iteration of development just before it begins.

Post-development testing

Post-development testing (black-box testing) takes place once the system is **complete**. This stage of testing is not concerned about individual algorithms, functions or procedures in the project. Post-development testing checks that the solution works and meets the requirements specification.

Post-development testing will often focus on qualitative testing. The speed, feel and accessibility of the software may all be tested in the post-development phase.

Stakeholders should also be involved at this stage. It is worth remembering that you will know the system very well by the time you have finished, so create tests that reflect the fact that stakeholders will not have seen this system before. Additionally, they may not be very computer literate. Tests you design for stakeholders should be written clearly and use simple language.

Testing using scenarios

Scenario testing is less defined than test plans, but a very valuable form of testing.

Imagine a system where a manager needs to log into a system to create a new client. They then need to book an appointment for them and send them a letter confirming this. These tests reflect the daily use the system would get.

To test this system, a set of scenarios could be created for stakeholders to follow. A scenario could be documented as follows:

Test scenario 1: **Manager** – user management
- Open the system
- Log in to the manager console
- Add a new client
- Create a new appointment for the client
- Send the letter to the client
- Save your changes
- Exit the system

An example post-development test scenario for a manager of the system

TIP   Creating a scenario with too much guidance can stop the stakeholder from making mistakes and giving you valuable feedback.

Test scenario 1: **Manager** – user management
- Open the system
- Log in to the manager console
  - UserName: aeinstein
  - Password: Apples!1
- Add a new client
  - Name: Elouise Brady
  - Address: 145 New Apartments, New Road, Aberdeen, AB99 0PA, UK
  - Phone: (07700) 900124
  - Email: ElouBrady@madeupemail.com
- Create a new appointment for the client
  - Tuesday 23rd August @ 08:45
- Send the letter to the client
- Save your changes
- Exit the system

An example post-development test scenario with data

Once the stakeholder has carried out the scenario tests, you will need to gain feedback from them. This feedback should find out the following:

1. What worked
2. What errors there were
3. How these errors impact the stakeholder
4. What areas for improvement they noticed
5. What their overall feel for the success of the system was

Chapter 5

The design

Other post-development testing may include a stakeholder agreeing that you have met certain requirements.

- Have you used the house style consistently?
- Does the GUI feel easy to use?
- Is important information clearly highlighted?

WARNING	Once you have created test plans, ensure that all requirements in the requirements specification have related tests to prove that they have been met. This will aid you in the Evaluation section.

TASK	Create test plans for the algorithms that you intend to implement. Remember that test plans can be created for each iteration of development just before it begins.

To do list
Have you done the following?

☐ **Broken down the problem into smaller parts which are easily solvable, and created a decomposition diagram, list or table showing the decomposition**

☐ **If using object-oriented programming, created a class diagram**

☐ **If using a database, created a data table for each table needed**

☐ **If using a database, created an Entity-Relationship (E-R) diagram**

☐ **If appropriate, created a Data Flow Diagram (DFD)**

☐ **Created algorithms that fully describe the solution**

☐ **Identified key variables and structures used in the system**

☐ **Drawn any GUI designs**

☐ **Discussed features that make the system more usable for the stakeholders**

☐ **Created test plans for algorithms and iterative development**

☐ **Created post-development test strategies, plans or scenarios**

☐ **Justify design decisions and test cases by linking back to the requirements specification**

Chapter 6
Software development

Objectives

- Plan and organise the software development
- Know when and how to record evidence
- Produce evidence of each stage of development
- Annotate code
- Produce evidence of testing at each iteration
- Produce evidence of failed tests along with how errors were fixed

Justifications

Before starting any development, it is advisable to create a plan. Organisation is key to completing the project before the deadline. There are two reasons why projects can fail in the development section:

1. Many students want to rush straight into producing code. They create a lot of code very quickly without testing regularly enough. This leads to issues when they attempt to debug their code. These students have often not spent enough time and thought in the Analysis section to understand what is required or to create a suitable structure. In some cases, the code needs to be re-written from scratch wasting even more time.

2. Other students fail to record their journey. For example, it is very easy to take a screenshot of development when an error occurs or a decision to change an algorithm is taken. It is, by contrast very hard to 'back track' to show development. Solutions often look reverse engineered and without the evidence being produced in the correct order, a poor mark may be awarded.

Software development

Organisation

In the Design section, your project will have been split up into key chunks, or iterations. If you have not already, it may be useful to use a simple level of project planning to help keep you on track. Planning the development will take an hour or two. However, a well thought out development plan will save you time and more, later in the project.

> **TIP** Having a plan for the development of your solution will let you know early if you have been too ambitious. You can then discuss your project with your teacher to see how you can catch up or alter what you are trying to achieve.

Project Iteration	Core Module	Sub Module	Dependency?	Week 1	Week 2	Week 3	Week 4	Week 5	Week 6
1	Movement	Up			Testing				
		Down							
		Left							
		Right							
2	Character	Health					Testing		
		Backpack							
		Location	Movement						
		Weapon							
		Armour							
3	Monster	Health						Testing	
		Life							
		Armour							
		Weapon							
		Location	Movement						
3	Maze	Character							
		Monsters							
		Walls							
		Doors							
		Traps							

A simple plan for the development of a solution

A simple plan like the one shown above can help focus on what needs to be done and how much time is available to complete it.

Remember that testing takes time and needs to be recorded. Also plan some contingency weeks that can be used to catch up if progress is behind schedule. Building in time to cope with delays will help you feel more confident if some parts take longer than originally planned.

> **TIP** Remember your plan is to help you organise your time. Whilst you can put it in your report, it is not specifically required by the mark scheme.

Recording the development

Recording evidence of the development is fundamental to proving your system works. Do not fall into the trap of recording everything in the smallest detail possible. A screenshot for every 20-30 lines of code may be enough. Some screenshots may be of a complete function or procedure. There is no rule, but in general focus on blocks of code and completed sections rather than line-by-line details.

Whichever method used to record the development of your solution, remember that quality is far more important than quantity.

Clearly laid out evidence that shows exactly what is needed will help a teacher to mark the work and help the moderator to find key evidence. It will also save you time when referring to different sections.

TIP	Over evidencing your development is often where time is wasted.

Evidence

There are a range of **evidence** methods that can be used to support your work. In some cases **photos** may work better than **screenshots**, but in other cases copying and pasting code may be clearest.

Video may also be used and may be a quick way of recording a particular error or solution that would be hard to describe.

You can save a lot of time by selecting the type of evidence you use carefully.

Screenshots

Screenshots are the easiest method of evidence recording. They can be created without additional software and are good for recording evidence of development for each iteration.

There are drawbacks to screenshots. The most overlooked one is that your documentation file size will increase significantly. This can make it slow to open and edit the report.

Screenshots may also need cropping and create problems with text wrapping in the word processor that is used.

Visibility of screenshots is key. Very often marks are lost as the screenshot's resolution is too low, or the size too small. This makes it unreadable. Unreadable screenshots cannot be given any marks.

An example of a screenshot where the text is too small to read

WARNING	Make sure that any screenshots allow the moderator to read it to avoid losing marks.

Chapter 6
Software development

Benefits	Drawbacks
• Quick to make • Do not require special software • Good at capturing development over time	• Usually needs cropping • Word wrapping and formatting • Potential for poor resolution • Shrinking screenshots can leave them unreadable • Taking too many screenshots will slow you down • Makes document file size large

Photos

Taking photos with a smartphone or a digital camera can also be an option. Photos may be more appropriate if you are working with physical computing solutions. For example, a photograph of a robot navigating a maze would be able to show distinct abilities far better than a screenshot of the computer code.

Photos will need to be transferred and cropped for the report. They share similar benefits and drawbacks to screenshots.

Note that for the majority of projects, photos are unlikely to be needed as screenshots are sufficient to show a program running on a display. However, for physical projects, or to show an end-user interacting with the product, photos may be the best form of evidence.

Benefits	Drawbacks
• Easy to take • Do not require special software • Can get good quality from modern smartphones • Good at capturing development over time • Generally easy to transfer to PC	• Usually need cropping/editing • File sizes from a modern smartphone tend to be large • Word wrapping and formatting • Shrinking photos of screens can leave text unreadable • Makes document file size large

Source code

Source code is a good way to show development. The code can be copied and pasted from an IDE quickly and efficiently. Copying and pasting will be better than taking screenshots. The text size can be increased or decreased in the word processor, and the file size of the report will remain small, which may make opening and editing faster.

If code is copied and pasted it will be clearer when printed. The moderator will also be able to zoom in if it is hard to read. This is not possible with a screenshot.

```
static float multiply(float num1, float num2)
{
    float result = num1 * num2;
    return result;
}
```

```
static float multiply(float num1, float num2)
{
    float result = num1 * num2;
    return result;
}
```

Text may be clearer if it is copied and pasted (left) rather than a screenshot (right)

There are times when a screenshot will work better, such as when showing feedback from the IDE.

Copying and pasting source code has some drawbacks. It can become hard to follow if it goes over a page. It may also cause a spell check to flag many errors, as it will not recognise the program syntax.

Auto-formatting within a word processor may also be a problem, making your code look like it does not work or has not been indented correctly. If you decide to copy and paste code then be careful to ensure that it appears as it would in the IDE.

Benefits	Drawbacks
• Very simple to copy and paste • IDE syntax highlighting will often be copied and pasted too • Keeps document size small • Changing to a small font is clearer than a scaled screenshot	• Hard to follow over multiple pages • Spellchecks do not like code • Formatting and syntax highlighting may change

Chapter 6
Software development

Annotation

Annotation of screenshots, source code or photos can be done in many ways. You can choose to annotate by the following methods:

1. Use image editing software
2. Use presentation software and then save as a JPEG or similar
3. Paste the image into word processing software and use drawing tools.

Method 1 is technically harder. Whilst the results are good, it takes time to do the annotation. It is therefore not advised unless the other methods are not appropriate.

Method 2 which uses presentation software such as Microsoft® PowerPoint® is easy to use, but it will often take longer than annotating directly in the report itself.

Method 3 tends to be the most popular and fastest. Be aware though that sometimes word processing packages can cause issues with layout. In this case, method 2 is advised.

> **TIP** When annotating with a word processor, remember to group all the objects together so that they move in the report as one object.

Good use of annotation can cut down the amount of writing you need to do.

```
static void Main(string[] args)
{
    int num1, num2;
    Console.WriteLine("A program to return the larger of two numbers");
    Console.Write("Please enter first number: ");
    num1 = int.Parse(Console.ReadLine());
    Console.Write("Please enter second number: ");
    num2 = int.Parse(Console.ReadLine());

    Console.WriteLine("The largest number is: " + Largest(num1, num2));
}

1 reference
static int Largest (int num1, int num2)
{
    if (num1 >= num2)
    {
        return num2;
    }
    else
    {
        return num2;
    }
}
```

When testing the function, the second number was always chosen as the largest number.

This was due to a logical error where num2 was being returned, not num1

Microsoft Visual Studio Debug Console
```
A program to return the larger of two numbers
Please enter first number: 78
Please enter second number: 5
The largest number is: 5
```

*An example of an annotated screenshot showing
the development and testing of a function. Continued on following page*

```
if (num1 >= num2)
{
    return num1;
}
```

Microsoft Visual Studio Debug Console

```
A program to return the larger of two numbers
Please enter first number: 78
Please enter second number: 5
The largest number is: 78
```

The program was tested with a new line of code which fixed the problem.

Annotation of screenshots or photos allows you to highlight key points in the evidence. Even adding A, B, C and so on to key areas will allow you to then use these as references within your write up.

Video

Video is a very powerful evidence tool, but it must be used with caution.

If a picture can tell 1,000 words, video can convey many more. Video can save you time taking multiple screenshots, each of which would need pasting, cropping and possibly editing.

Video is perfect for showing movement in games or transitions through a complex system. It can also record sound. Therefore, if there are spoken elements in the GUI then this would be a good way to show it working.

Remember that videos will need editing. The software to record and capture video is generally free, but you need to be confident in using it.

Most modern smartphones record video and this is a good option to consider.

Video file size is something to be careful of. Sixty seconds of video should be enough to show key tests working. There is a balance between purpose and appropriateness of a video versus screenshots.

> **TIP**
> If you use video as evidence, be sure to name your videos clearly, and use timestamps in the video to point to exactly where the evidence is.

Benefits	Drawbacks
• Shows transition and movement • Very suited to games • Can save a lot of time over screenshot evidence • Screen recording software can be free	• Can generate large files • Harder to reference • Must timestamp every reference • Not 'in the document' so must be clear where you are using video as evidence

Chapter 6
Software development

Using tables

It is possible to use tables to layout evidence. This reduces the chance of formatting issues to do with word wrapping.

Using tables can be useful if there are many screenshots to fit on each page. This may be most relevant in the testing evidence that will be generated.

```static void Main(string[] args)\n{\n Console.WriteLine("Testing multiply function");\n //Test 1\n Console.WriteLine(multiply(1, 2));\n //Test 2\n Console.WriteLine(multiply(1, "text"));\n //Test 3\n Console.WriteLine(multiply(1, 2.5f));\n //Test 4\n Console.WriteLine(multiply(1, -2));\n //Test 5\n Console.WriteLine(multiply(1, null));\n Console.ReadLine();\n}\n\n5 references\nstatic float multiply(float num1, float num2)\n{\n float result = num1 * num2;\n return result;\n}```	• This is a screenshot of the tests for the multiply function that I wrote in my code • The IDE picked up two errors that prevented the code from compiling • Any inputs to the multiply function must be floats. Therefore, if the input comes from a user, it must be validated and then converted from a string to a float • These tests were commented out so that Test 1, Test 3 and Test 4 could be run
```Testing multiply function\n2\n2.5\n-2```	• This is the output of the tests showing that all passed successfully

> **TIP** Text in any screenshots must be easily legible. You may wish to rotate pages to landscape for this section of your report.

It is, of course, down to personal preference as to which method of laying out evidence you choose.

74

Overview

Working out what needs to be evidenced and how to present it is a key skill. Your teacher and moderator will need clear evidence that the system is working as intended.

The Development section needs to show a review after each iteration of your solution. It is essential that the evidence in the Development and Testing sections shows that the requirements of the system have been met. Equally, you must explain what you did and justify any decisions that were taken.

The Development section also needs to highlight core techniques that make the system appropriate for an A Level project.

Key techniques that show good programming technique and structure need to be demonstrated in your code. This will include:

- Modular development
- Annotation of the code
- Meaningful variable names
- Validation
- Use of OOP if appropriate
- Use of appropriate data structures for storing data
- Error handling
- Showing how you moved between prototypes/iterations in your code

TASK

During or at the end of each iteration, add evidence to your Development section including the following :

- Evidence of the code produced
- Relate the code produced to the decomposition in the Analysis section
- Explain what you did and justify the decisions you took
- Provide evidence of prototype versions of the solution at this stage
- Annotate the code
- Show that variables and data structures have been correctly named
- Show evidence of error handling and validation
- Show how you moved between prototypes/iterations
- Focus on the significant challenges you faced
- Avoid writing about every small issue encountered
- Review the development of this iteration

Chapter 6
Software development

Testing

Introduction

Remember that there are two testing processes. Iterative testing is carried out during each iteration and post-development testing is carried out after all development has been completed. Each should be documented separately in order to make it clear that you have done both. Post-development testing is covered in the next chapter.

For each iteration, or testing review that is carried out, add clear headings in the Development for Iterative tests.

> **TIP** Make references within your work as clear as possible for your teacher and the moderator. The easier your evidence is to find, the quicker they can award marks.

The core principle of evidencing testing is to prove your system works. This does not mean that every test you do has to be evidenced with a screenshot.

You should include tests to cover the following, at each iteration:
- Overview of tests which were successful
- A focus on failed tests and corrective action taken
- Evidence to show that your system is robust
- Enough evidence to prove that your system is functional

Tests that show errors and corrective action give much more evidence for a working system than a page of screen shots that only shows valid tests.

Iterative testing

Testing iteratively can be done at any time during an iteration and does not always have to be after you have written all of the code.

Remember that when you compile and run the program, you are **already** carrying out testing. At this stage you should record what has been tested and check appropriate test cases.

Failed tests show solid development strategy and understanding. No one writes a perfect piece of complex software correctly at the first try. The exam board knows that there will be errors and issues encountered along the way.

> **TIP** Repeating lots of tests which are all successful will unnecessarily add to your workload and have minimal impact to the report's quality.

Strong iterative testing features

Strong iterative testing will have the following features:

- Summarise the tests which worked using a range of suitable evidence
- Demonstrate a few of the tests which have passed, focusing on the more interesting ones or the ones that show the system has met a requirement in the requirements specification
- Provide more detailed evidence of non-trivial failed tests
- Discuss the reason why tests failed, showing a clear line of thought to a solution
- Show the implementation of the solution
- Prove the error has been fixed

Evidencing testing

Tables can be a very useful way of recording test evidence. You will probably have created a test plan earlier using a table.

ID	Pass/Fail	Comment	Evidence
1			
2			
3			
4			
5			

Example test results table

Copy and paste the tests you need from your earlier planning to the point in the report where they are actually tested. Then add columns to the copied table or beneath it.

The columns need to show clearly if the test passed or failed. It is beneficial to highlight tests that fail in red and tests that pass in green. Any tests that fail need to be fixed with evidence of solution and evidence of the test being carried out again successfully.

Comments can be added to tests. There is no need to write obvious comments such as "It didn't work". Instead, add comments where they show understanding. For instance, "It appears that there is a logic error that occurs here when the function is called with large values." shows that an idea has already been considered for what may be causing the error.

> **TIP**
>
> Avoid focusing on trivial errors. Instead you should hone in on interesting errors that were a challenge to solve. For example, getting a library to work, ensuring a text file reads the right character set or spending a long time to find that an object was being passed by value rather than reference. These are all examples of interesting errors and problems where detail can be given about how they were solved. This will help keep your documentation succinct and clear.

Completing the evidence column

Pasting screenshots into a table can cause issues. Often there is a temptation to shrink them to fit. This makes the screenshot hard to read, and the evidence becomes useless.

If you need more space, put the evidence after the table and refer to it in the box, e.g. "See Screenshot 34". Remember, evidence must be clear to read for the moderator.

Fixing errors

If you can, fix any errors that are found. If you cannot, try to work around them. Link the impact back to your requirements specification. When errors are critical to the system working it is worth taking the time to find solutions.

For minor errors that don't really impact the system, log them and move on. You can always come back to them later if you have time.

> **TIP** Leaving minor errors in the solution can save you time in your project. Make sure that these errors don't impact later development.

Revising designs, tests and code

Some errors may require you to redesign your solution. Do not worry – this is expected.

Be clear when you have a test failure that causes you to feel that a redesign for part of the system is needed. Ask these questions:

1. Is the error down to poor code design, or a simple mistake?
2. Will the error cause a significant impact on my system?
3. Does the code need re-writing because of this?

If 'Yes' is the answer to all of these, then:

- For small edits: Discuss the changes made to the pseudocode in a short paragraph and evidence the altered code. Finally, re-run the test(s).
- Large edits: Re-write the pseudocode, document the changes, edit the code and evidence the changes. Finally, re-run the test(s).

Updating test tables

When code is restructured or re-written, tests may need to be changed. These should be recorded. The easiest way to do this is to copy and paste the original tests, discuss the changes and show the updated test table.

> **TIP** Iterative development is fluid. Making changes along the way is fine. Just make sure to document these clearly. Include justification as to why you made the changes.

TASK During or at the end of each iteration, add evidence to your Development section to show that testing has taken place, including any tests that have failed, how they have been fixed and a justification for any actions taken.

To do list
Have you done the following?

☐ Planned the software development

☐ For each iteration, shown evidence of the code produced

☐ For each iteration, explained what you did and justified any decisions you made

☐ For each iteration, given evidence of prototype versions of your solution

☐ Made sure that code is well structured and modular

☐ Annotated all code

☐ Named all variables and structures appropriately

☐ Used validation for all key elements of the solution

☐ Reviewed progress at each iteration

☐ For each iteration, carried out testing

☐ Given evidence of any tests that have failed and shown how they were fixed

Chapter 7
Evaluation

Objectives

- Produce evidence of post development testing
- Give evidence of usability testing
- Cross reference test evidence with success criteria
- Explain how any criteria that hasn't been met could be met with further development
- Justify the success of usability features
- Explain how any unmet usability features could be met with further development
- Discuss maintenance of the system
- Describe any improvements that could be made to the program and how any limitations could be overcome with further development

Success of the solution

It is essential that in the final post development testing and evaluation the system is cross referenced against the success criteria. This is crucial in showing that the system works. Don't worry if some parts do not work fully. You do not have to have a 100% perfect project to score full marks for this section.

What you must do is clearly link your evaluation back to your requirements.

Effective evaluation = Stakeholder requirements + test evidence + critical review

Post-development testing

Before an evaluation of the system can be carried out, the finished system must be fully tested. This testing looks at the system as a whole. The tests that need to be carried out will have been created earlier in the Design section.

Remember that most of the program such as modules, classes and algorithms will have already been tested as part of the iterative testing. The focus of the post development testing is to show that everything works together as one robust unit.

These tests should be similar to how a stakeholder may use the system. Whilst you will have an intimate experience of how your system was built, you need to put yourself in the stakeholder's shoes for the purposes of post development testing.

Post-development testing needs to confirm that all the stakeholder requirements and success criteria have been met. These will have been listed in the Analysis section.

Strong post development testing features

Strong post development testing will have the following features:

- Avoid repeating any of the iterative tests already carried out
- Focus on the system as a whole, and not individual parts
- Mimic real-life user interactions
- Directly link to the original requirements in the requirements specification to show if, how and to what extent they have been met

Remember that all testing evidence needs to cross-reference the success criteria in the requirements specification. It is helpful to list all the requirements and success criteria in a table and then either provide evidence for it being met or refer back to another page in the report that provides this evidence.

> **TIP** Qualitative testing needs to be done by the stakeholders. At this stage focus on quantitative testing.

> **TASK** Carry out any quantitative post-development testing.

Usability and stakeholder testing

Once all of the quantitative testing has been completed, you need to show that the qualitative criteria have been met. This will help to show that the system is usable by the stakeholder. This type of testing is known as Usability Testing. Check that the usability features that were identified in the Analysis have been tested and cross-referenced.

Stakeholder testing is much better done through realistic scenarios. The scenarios that were created in the Design section can now be given to your stakeholders for feedback.

For qualitative feedback, a questionnaire could be used with questions such as "Rate the responsiveness of the system". Alternatively, a meeting with your stakeholders could allow you to ask how they feel usability and qualitative success criteria have been met.

Strong usability testing features

Strong usability and stakeholder testing will have the following features:

- Avoid repeating any tests previously carried out
- Give evidence of the stakeholder carrying out tests
- Evaluate stakeholder feedback
- Discuss both good points and weaknesses
- Clearly show you have thought about the impact on the stakeholders

If you feel that usability could be improved, refer to the improvements in the 'Further Development' section.

An overall summary of your usability features is often a good way to draw things together. Discuss aspects of usability from the point of view of the stakeholders of the system. If the system has an impact on clients, discuss this as well.

For example, it may be that having a simply organised menu system allows faster order processing. This has clear benefits to the stakeholders such as taking less time to record orders, the ability to take more orders over a set time and less likelihood of making errors. There are also positive outcomes for customers. They will receive their orders faster and with fewer errors which will result in improved customer satisfaction.

 Complete the usability testing. Include evidence from your stakeholders where appropriate.

Incomplete systems

There may be occasions where some features or aspects of the system do not work as intended. This may be for a range of reasons.

Incomplete solutions can still achieve high marks. Do not worry if some elements have proven more challenging to develop. What is important is that these issues are highlighted. Where problems have been encountered, discuss why they happened, how they will affect the system, and potentially how they could be addressed with further development.

Try to get stakeholder feedback on these issues. This will then give you more to discuss as part of your evaluation.

TASK Comment on any success criteria that you haven't managed to meet.

Effective evaluation

If you have numbered your requirements specification and test evidence, then this will make the Evaluation section a lot easier to write. It will also keep it clear and easy to follow.

You must refer to each of your requirements systematically when you write the evaluation.

Avoid the temptation of copying and pasting a lot of screenshots or code into your evaluation. If you have tested it already, refer back to it. This will save you time and reduce the amount of work to be done.

The evaluation must be critical. Being honest and open will give you more to write about. Errors and bugs are fine to discuss and will help in considering maintenance issues, limitations of the solution and further development.

"One issue I had was in implementing the automatic scheduling for the restaurant tables. Whilst this worked, it did not accurately work out the number of staff as well as I had wanted. There was a rounding error that I could not trace, and this left some days being short of a member of staff (see tests 14,15 and 18).

I discussed this with the manager (See Questionnaire 2, question 5). They said that this was not ideal, but that they usually checked the schedules by hand anyway. They felt they would still save time with my system, even though it is not as effective as it could be.

Usability is still much better than their previous system (See Questionnaire 2, question 6).

A further development I could make here is to investigate another algorithm to calculate the staffing rota which would improve the functionality of this section."

An example of part of an effective critical evaluation

Maintenance

It is important to show consideration of the maintenance of the system that has been developed. Examples that may be discussed include how to back-up the system, how to implement upgrades and any other suggestions for routine procedures that need to be carried out to make sure that the system works day to day.

The amount that needs to be written for this section will depend on the particular project undertaken. In many cases this is not likely to require a large amount of writing, but it must be included for every project.

Here are some ideas to consider writing about:
- How portable is the system?
- Will the system need updates?
- What about data storage and back up needs?
- Does the data in the system need archiving?
- Are there any future technology developments that could be considered?

> **TASK**   Discuss in the report how your system will be maintained.

Further development

Further development looks at potential ways to either improve your system further or reflect back on the 'would be nice to have' features that were identified in the Analysis section.

Ideas that should be covered include:

- What new features would improve the system if it were further developed in the future?
- If there was more time, what would I have included?
- What works, but could be improved?

This is a good opportunity to raise questions with your stakeholders and allow them to make suggestions as to how the system could be improved. This will provide evidence for your final suggestions.

This section does not need to be long. A few well written paragraphs will often be enough. However, it is important to include this section.

> **TASK**   Discuss how your system can be further improved.

To do list
Have you done the following?

- [ ] Provided annotated evidence of post development testing
- [ ] Provided annotated evidence of usability testing
- [ ] Gained feedback from stakeholders
- [ ] Cross referenced evidence with success criteria
- [ ] Reviewed how any unmet criteria and usability features could be improved in future development
- [ ] Justified the success of usability features
- [ ] Discussed how the system will be maintained in the future
- [ ] Discussed potential improvements

Chapter 8
Final checks

Objectives

- Review your project and report against the mark scheme
- Ensure the report is laid out well
- Check for referencing and third party material
- Ensure that the report has been proof-read

Checking evidence in the report

> **TIP**
>
> The following suggestions show ideas for how you can check you have met all the criteria on the mark scheme. Whilst you don't have to do these, you may find it useful for making sure that you have covered everything needed in the report. Choose the method that works best for you.

Compare against checklists

First check that you have carried out all the tasks in this book. Then go through each of the to do lists and make sure you have carried out each item. Check off each one as a record of completion. The tasks have been closely aligned to what is needed in the mark scheme.

Compare against the mark scheme

Now is the time to take a clean copy of the mark scheme and to check that you have covered all areas given in it.

Chapter 8
Final checks

You may find it useful to pretend you are the marker. Create a table, similar to the one below:

Section	Mark Scheme	Evidence (pg.)	Completed
Analysis	Requirement 1	2, 5, 6	Yes
	Requirement 2	4, 5, 8	Improve
	Requirement 3	3, 4, 5	Yes
Design	Requirement 1	7, 10	Yes
	Requirement 2	8. 9	Yes
	Requirement 3	8, 10	Yes
Development	Requirement 1	2, 5, 6	Improve
	Requirement 2	4, 5, 8	Improve

An example of how to check that evidence required by the mark scheme has been met

> **TIP** Your teacher may have created a version of the mark scheme for you to use. Check you understand what is required at each section before starting this process.

Log where you believe that you have met each mark scheme statement then record the page numbers in the report. This will help to prove to your teacher that you have the required evidence. It will also enable you to see if you may have missed anything.

If you think that you could do some extra work in any section, mark it down for improvement. Your teacher can then give you some generic feedback as to whether you could develop any sections you have highlighted. For instance, they may say that your usability testing needs to be developed in order to satisfy the criteria of the top mark band. However, they cannot tell you exactly what to do to improve.

An alternative way to check your work against the mark scheme is to simply use a highlighter with a printed copy of the requirements. Read each section and highlight any parts that you can find good evidence for. At the end of this process, any areas that are not highlighted need more evidence.

Always consider the time needed to add more evidence against the marks which will be gained. Spending ten hours to gain a couple of marks in the Design section will not be as effective as spending three hours working on a missing post-development testing section which may be worth many more marks.

> **TASK** Compare your report against the criteria given in the mark scheme.

Documentation and evidence

Your documentation is essential for success in the project and proving your system works. Information should be presented in a logically structured manner.

It is worth spending some time reviewing the layout. The following checks should be carried out on your documentation:

- Each page has a suitable header and footer containing:
  - Candidate name
  - Candidate number
  - Centre name
  - Centre number
  - Project title
  - Page number
- The table of contents has been updated
- Each section has a clear heading and relates to part of the mark scheme
- Sub-headings are used effectively
- Screenshots are readable and clear
- References to evidence are accurate
- Wording is clear and concise
- Referencing is complete and accurate

Proof-reading and referencing

Proof-reading

A **spellchecker** is usually an in-built component of the word processing package that has been used. Make sure you use it to help find any errors. Submitting work with poor spelling and grammar gives a bad impression.

Remember that spellcheckers will not catch all errors so be sure to leave time to read your work at least once from beginning to end. Confusing wording or inaccurate use of terminology can lose you marks if they cause the moderator to misunderstand what is being said.

TASK	Proof-read and spellcheck your report.

Chapter 8

Final checks

Referencing

Not referencing sources that you have used is considered cheating. If you are found to have used sources, and not referenced them, then you may receive zero marks for your work or be stopped from taking your A Level completely.

Markers and moderators must be able to see the following:

- What has been copied or come from another source
- That the source has been acknowledged
- Where/how you have developed the source material into your own project or words

Your school or the exam board may use plagiarism checkers. These are sophisticated in flagging up areas of reports or projects that have been copied.

 TASK   Make sure you have included a references section and all sources have been correctly referenced.

Submitting the project

Ask your teacher how they would like the report, project files and any other resources such as videos to be submitted. If you forget to give files to your teacher, then you may well lose marks. You may need to print the report or provide an electronic version. Be aware of any deadlines that your teacher has given and make sure you submit your work well before the deadline.

To do list
Have you done the following?

- [ ] Reviewed your project and report against the mark scheme
- [ ] Compared your work against the mark scheme to identify any areas that aren't complete or need improvement
- [ ] Completed any missing parts of the report if needed
- [ ] Made any improvements if needed
- [ ] Proofread and spell checked the report
- [ ] Ensured all references to other sources are included
- [ ] Prepared your report and other files in the correct format requested by your teacher ready for submitting
- [ ] Submitted your report and any other files requested before the deadline

Index

Appendix
Useful shortcuts and key combinations

Editing shortcut key combinations

Ctrl + A	Select all
Ctrl + B	Apply or remove bold formatting
Ctrl + C	Copy
Ctrl + Shift + C	Copy formatting
Ctrl + F	Find
Ctrl + I	Apply or remove italic formatting
Ctrl + P	Print
Ctrl + S	Save
Ctrl + V	Paste
Ctrl + Shift + V	Paste formatting
Ctrl + X	Cut
Ctrl + Y	Redo or repeat last action
Ctrl + Z	Undo an action
Shift + F3	Toggle case
Alt + =	Insert equation
Shift + Enter	Create a soft line break
Ctrl + Enter	Insert a page break
Ctrl + [	Decrease font size
Ctrl +]	Increase font size

Navigation shortcuts

Ctrl + Home	Go to beginning of document
Ctrl + End	Go to end of document
Shift + F5	Go to last place text was edited